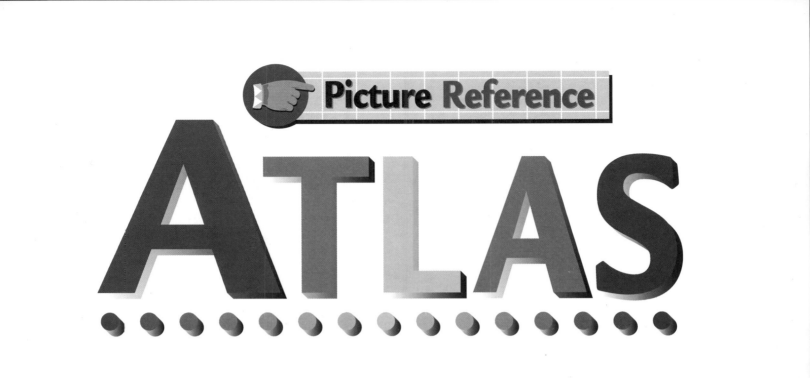

Picture Reference
ATLAS

MEL PICKERING

WORLD BOOK / TWO-CAN

Text Andrew Solway
Consultant Steve Watts
Computer illustrations Mel Pickering, Jacqueline Land
Editors Deborah Kespert, Kate Asser
Editorial support Claire Llewellyn, Julia Hillyard, Claire Yude
Art director Belinda Webster
Senior designer Helen Holmes
Photographic credits Zefa p7, John Englefield p9

First published in the United States in 1996 by
World Book, Inc.
525 W. Monroe
20th Floor
Chicago
IL USA 60661
in association with Two-Can Publishing Ltd.

Copyright © Two-Can Publishing Ltd., 1996

**For information on other Word Book products,
call 1-800-255-1750, x 2238.**

ISBN: 0-7166-1746-3 (pbk.)
ISBN: 0-7166-1745-5 (hbk.)
LC: 96-60464

Printed in Hong Kong

1 2 3 4 5 6 7 8 9 10 99 98 97 96

Contents

What is an atlas?

An atlas is a book of maps showing different parts of the world. Maps are small pictures of big places drawn from above. They can show somewhere as small as a village or as big as the world. You can use atlases and maps in all sorts of ways. They might show you how to find your way around, or tell you what a place is like.

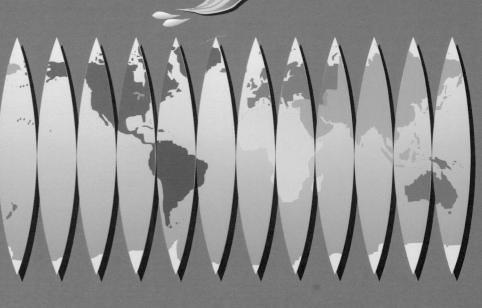

1 One of the most difficult maps to draw is one showing all of the world. This is because the world is round, like a huge ball, but maps are flat. Imagine painting the world onto the skin of an orange.

2 You could carefully peel the skin into segments.

3 Then you could lay the peel flat to make a map of the world.

4 Mapmakers fill the gaps by stretching some parts of the map and shrinking others.

On this map, you can see that more than half of the Earth is covered by four big oceans. The rest of the Earth is divided into seven huge areas of land, called continents. There are also three imaginary lines on the map. The equator circles the Earth's center. The Arctic Circle is at the top of the Earth and the Antarctic Circle is at the bottom.

ARCTIC OCEAN

Arctic Circle

EUROPE

ASIA

PACIFIC OCEAN

NORTH AMERICA

ATLANTIC OCEAN

AFRICA

Equator

INDIAN OCEAN

SOUTH AMERICA

AUSTRALIA

Antarctic Circle

ANTARCTICA

1 This is a picture of a house on the corner of Park Street, which runs through a seaside town. You can see the hedge around the house, the tree outside and some of the street, but you cannot see the town or the sea because the picture is not big enough to show all these details.

2 This map shows Park Street from above. It shows less detail but a bigger area than before. Can you spot the house on the corner? Here, Park Street measures 4 inches (10cm), but it is really 1 mile (1km) long. This means that on the map every 4 inches (10cm) is the same as 1 mile (1km) in the real place. This is called *scale*.

Park Street

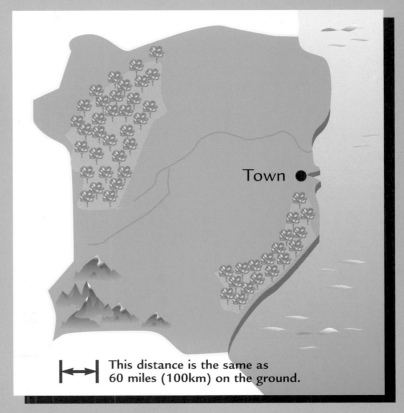

This distance is the same as 60 miles (100km) on the ground.

Town ●

3 This map shows a bigger area than the last map because it has a smaller scale. It shows all of the town. You cannot see the houses or all the streets, but you can see Park Street. On this map, Park Street is 2 inches (5cm) long. This means every 2 inches (5cm) on the map is the same as 1 mile (1km) in the real place.

4 This map shows the country where the town is found. The town is shown as a dot. The scale bar tells you that $3/8$ inch (1cm) on the map is the same as 60 miles (100km) in the real place. In this atlas, each map has a different scale and scale bar. On pages 10-11 you can see all the whole world at the same scale.

Hot and cold

Around the world, there are different patterns of weather called climates. The climate of a country depends on where it is in the world. It is always hot near the equator and cold near the North and South Poles. On each map in this atlas, you will find a locator globe, showing you where countries and continents are in the world. The globe has arrows pointing to the four directions— north, south, east and west.

The sun warms all the countries in the world, but shines more strongly on some than others. These countries have the warmest weather. Around the world, the weather also changes at different times of year.

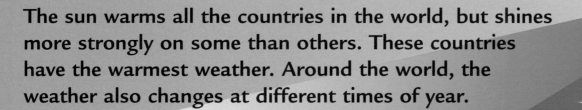

Arctic Circle

Tropic of Cancer

Equator

Tropic of Capricorn

Around the North and South Poles, the sun is never high in the sky and shines weakly, so the land is always cold, especially in winter.

Near the equator, the sun shines strongest and directly from above. Here the climate is hot, with wet and dry seasons.

Above and below the equator, there are two imaginary lines called the Tropic of Cancer and the Tropic of Capricorn. Countries between the tropics and the North and South Poles have warm summers and cold winters.

Different climates suit particular kinds of plants, and make different types of land for animals and people to live in. If a place has a rainy climate, lots of plants grow. If the climate is dry, fewer and different plants grow.

On the map below and the maps in this atlas, different types of land are shown by small pictures, called symbols, and colors. These photographs show you what the land really looks like.

Usually, the poles are icy cold. In summer, a few small plants grow around the Arctic.

Deciduous forests grow in cool areas. The trees lose their leaves in autumn.

Evergreen trees stay green all year. Evergreen forests grow in cold places.

Grassland includes tropical savanna (seen here), farmland and flat plains, called pampas.

Only the toughest plants and animals are able to survive in dry deserts.

Thick, green rainforests grow where it is warm and wet all year.

Few plants grow on rocky mountains, which are often covered in snow.

Arctic Circle

Tropic of Cancer

Equator

Tropic of Capricorn

This map shows different types of land found in the world.

Antarctic Circle

About this atlas

The maps in this atlas can tell you an enormous amount about the places they show. Look carefully at the pictures to find out more.

Each country is run from a capital city. These are shown by the flag of the country and a star.

A gray line shows a country border. When countries are arguing about a border or are not sure where the border is, the line is dotted.

A blue line shows a river. The name of the river is written alongside. Rivers can run through many countries.

Crops grow all over the world. Look out for wheat, rice, fruit and vegetables. You may see coffee, tea and sugar cane, too.

Some buildings are shown on the maps. You may see a famous monument, an old ruin or a type of home.

This picture shows where people drill into the land and seabed for oil, which is used to power all kinds of machines.

Different kinds of animals live in different parts of the world. Look for animals that live in the sea, on land and in the air.

This picture shows where people mine for diamonds. People also mine coal, silver, jewels, gold, copper, tin and iron.

Different people live around the world. Look for people playing sport or enjoying a traditional dance.

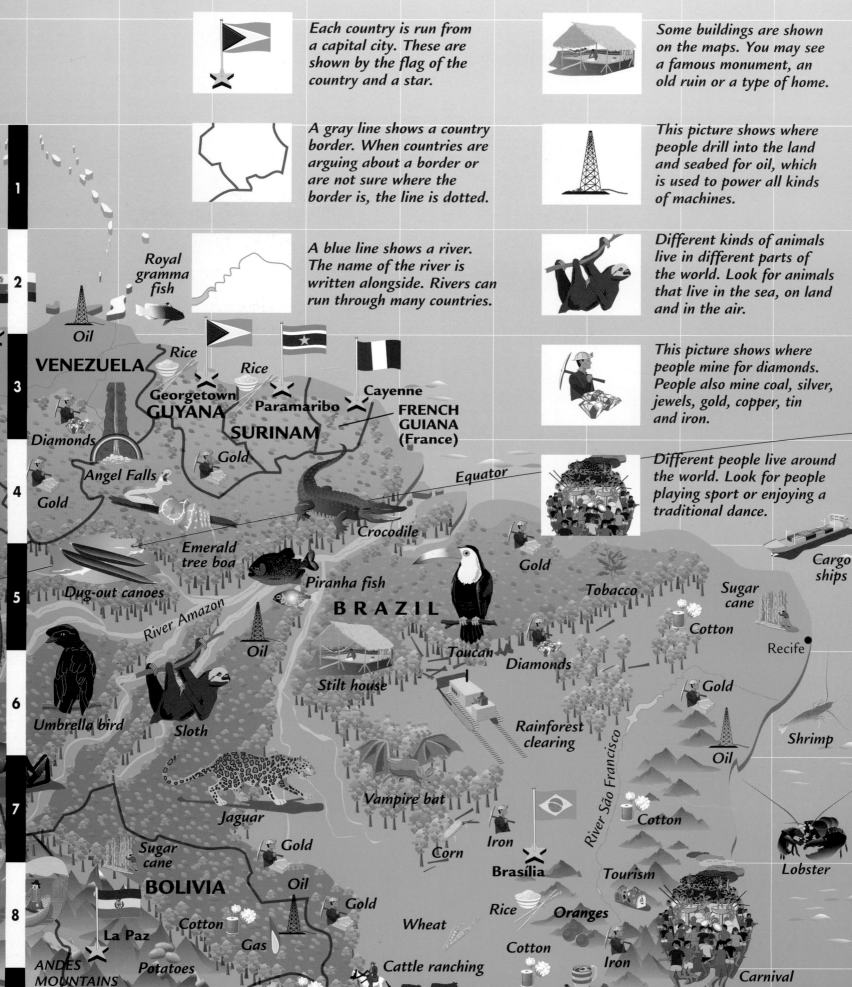

About the Factfile

Each map has a Factfile with facts about the places you can see. You might find out about a special animal or plant from a particular part of the world. Look at the picture beside each fact and then find it on the map. The facts in this Factfile are about the map of part of South America shown on the opposite page. Can you find all the pictures on the map?

On page 42, you will find a section of fascinating facts, full of many interesting things about the countries of the world.

Factfile

 South America is home to nearly one quarter of all known animals and around 2,500 different kinds of trees.

 The longest mountain range in the world is the Andes in South America.

Half of all the people in South America live in Brazil.

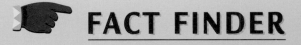

FACT FINDER

Each map has a grid, which divides it into squares. The columns run up and down and have letters. The rows run from side to side and have numbers. This means each square has a name, or grid reference.

The Fact Finder asks questions about places on the map. You can find the answers by looking at the grid reference.

Here is a Fact Finder question about the map of part of South America shown on the opposite page.

▶ What is the name of the highest waterfall in the world? (See square E 4.)

To find square E 4, lay your ruler on column E, at the bottom of the map. Leave the ruler lying on the map. Now put your finger on row 4, at the side of the map. Run your finger along row 4 in a straight line. Square E 4 is where your finger meets the ruler.

You should have found Angel Falls which is in Venezuela.

▼ This girl is answering the Fact Finder question. She is using a ruler and her finger to find the correct grid reference.

World map

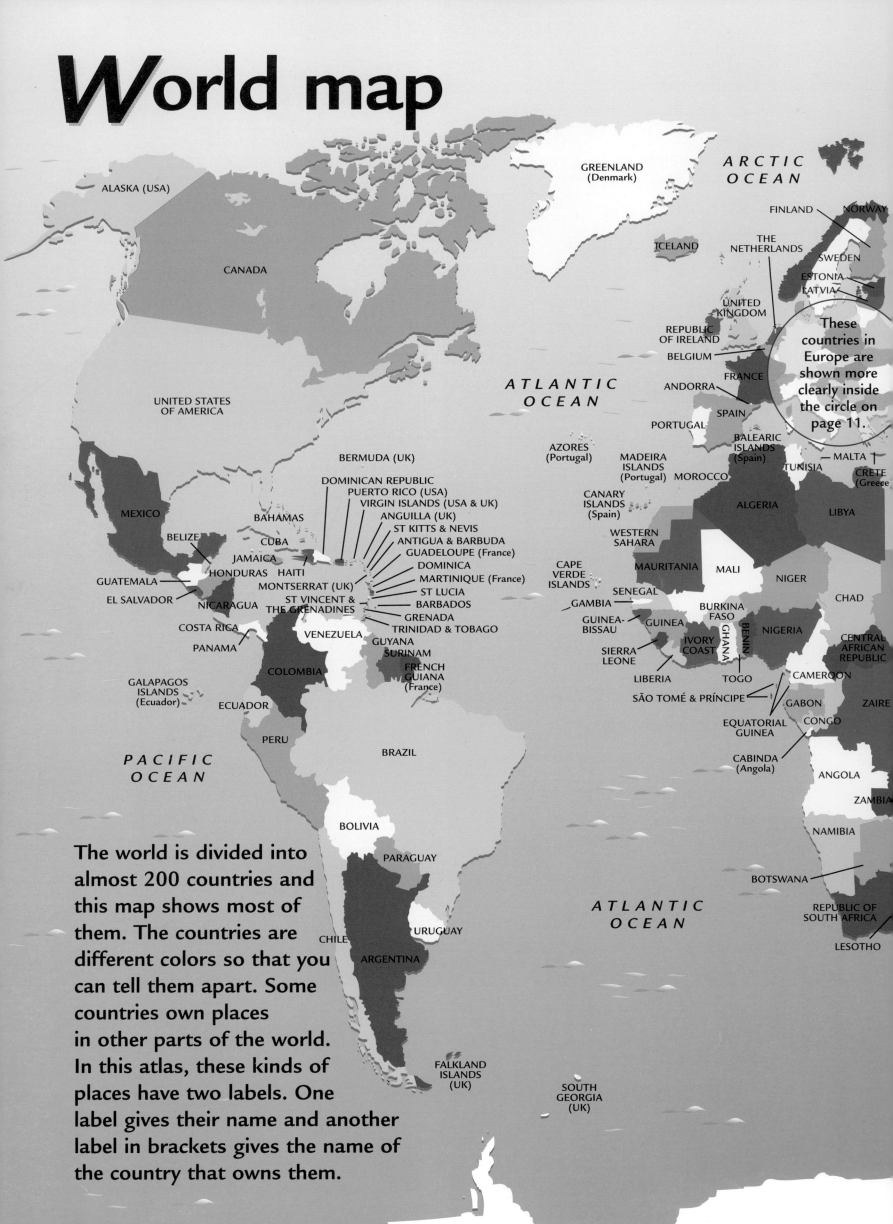

GREENLAND
(Denmark)

ARCTIC
OCEAN

ALASKA (USA)

CANADA

ICELAND

FINLAND   NORWAY

THE
NETHERLANDS   SWEDEN

ESTONIA
LATVIA

UNITED
KINGDOM

REPUBLIC
OF IRELAND

BELGIUM

ANDORRA

FRANCE

These
countries
in Europe are
shown more
clearly inside
the circle on
page 11.

ATLANTIC
OCEAN

UNITED STATES
OF AMERICA

PORTUGAL

SPAIN

BALEARIC
ISLANDS
(Spain)

MALTA

TUNISIA

CRETE
(Greece

BERMUDA (UK)

AZORES
(Portugal)

MADEIRA
ISLANDS
(Portugal)

MOROCCO

ALGERIA

LIBYA

MEXICO

BELIZE

CUBA

JAMAICA

DOMINICAN REPUBLIC
PUERTO RICO (USA)
VIRGIN ISLANDS (USA & UK)
ANGUILLA (UK)
ST KITTS & NEVIS
ANTIGUA & BARBUDA
GUADELOUPE (France)
DOMINICA
MARTINIQUE (France)
ST LUCIA
BARBADOS
GRENADA
TRINIDAD & TOBAGO

BAHAMAS

CANARY
ISLANDS
(Spain)

WESTERN
SAHARA

CAPE
VERDE
ISLANDS

MAURITANIA

MALI

NIGER

CHAD

GUATEMALA

HONDURAS   HAITI

MONTSERRAT (UK)

ST VINCENT &
THE GRENADINES

GAMBIA

SENEGAL

GUINEA-
BISSAU

GUINEA

BURKINA
FASO

NIGERIA

CENTRAL
AFRICAN
REPUBLIC

EL SALVADOR

NICARAGUA

COSTA RICA

PANAMA

VENEZUELA

GUYANA

SURINAM

FRENCH
GUIANA
(France)

SIERRA
LEONE

IVORY
COAST

GHANA

BENIN

TOGO

LIBERIA

COLOMBIA

GALAPAGOS
ISLANDS
(Ecuador)

ECUADOR

PERU

BRAZIL

SÃO TOMÉ & PRÍNCIPE

EQUATORIAL
GUINEA

GABON

CONGO

CAMEROON

ZAIRE

CABINDA
(Angola)

ANGOLA

PACIFIC
OCEAN

ZAMBIA

NAMIBIA

BOLIVIA

PARAGUAY

BOTSWANA

ATLANTIC
OCEAN

REPUBLIC OF
SOUTH AFRICA

LESOTHO

The world is divided into
almost 200 countries and
this map shows most of
them. The countries are
different colors so that you
can tell them apart. Some
countries own places
in other parts of the world.
In this atlas, these kinds of
places have two labels. One
label gives their name and another
label in brackets gives the name of
the country that owns them.

CHILE

URUGUAY

ARGENTINA

FALKLAND
ISLANDS
(UK)

SOUTH
GEORGIA
(UK)

ANTARCTICA

RUSSIA

KAZAKHSTAN

UKRAINE
AZERBAIJAN
ARMENIA
GEORGIA
TURKEY
CYPRUS
SYRIA
LEBANON
IRAQ
JORDAN
ISRAEL
EGYPT
SUDAN

UZBEKISTAN
KYRGYZSTAN
TURKMENISTAN
TAJIKISTAN
AFGHANISTAN
IRAN
KUWAIT
BAHRAIN
QATAR
UNITED
ARAB
EMIRATES
SAUDI
ARABIA
OMAN
PAKISTAN

MONGOLIA

CHINA

NORTH
KOREA
SOUTH
KOREA

JAPAN

PACIFIC
OCEAN

BHUTAN
NEPAL
INDIA
BANGLADESH

MACAO
(Portugal)

TAIWAN
(China)

MYANMAR

LAOS

HONG
KONG
(UK)

NORTHERN
MARIANAS
(USA)

ERITREA   YEMEN
DJIBOUTI

ETHIOPIA

SOCOTRA
(Yemen)

MALDIVE
ISLANDS

ANDAMAN
ISLANDS
(India)

NICOBAR
ISLANDS
(India)

SRI
LANKA

THAILAND
CAMBODIA

VIETNAM

GUAM (USA)

MARSHALL
ISLANDS

PHILIPPINES

PALAU
(USA)

BRUNEI

STATES OF MICRONESIA

UGANDA
KENYA

SOMALIA

SEYCHELLES

INDIAN
OCEAN

SINGAPORE

MALAYSIA

NAURU

KIRIBATI

RWANDA
BURUNDI
TANZANIA   MALAWI
COMOROS
MAYOTTE (France)

MADAGASCAR

INDONESIA

IRIAN JAYA
(Indonesia)

PAPUA NEW
GUINEA

SOLOMON
ISLANDS

TUVALU

ZIMBABWE

MOZAMBIQUE

SWAZILAND

AUSTRALIA

VANUATU

FIJI

NEW
CALEDONIA
(France)

SWEDEN
DENMARK

GERMANY

LUXEMBOURG

LIECHTENSTEIN

SWITZERLAND

MONACO

CORSICA
(France)

SARDINIA
(Italy)

LATVIA
LITHUANIA
(Russia)

POLAND

BELARUS

CZECH
REPUBLIC
SLOVAKIA

AUSTRIA
SLOVENIA

SAN
MARINO

ITALY

VATICAN
CITY

HUNGARY

CROATIA

UKRAINE

MOLDOVA

ROMANIA

FEDERAL
REPUBLIC OF
YUGOSLAVIA

BOSNIA-
HERZEGOVINA

ALBANIA

GREECE

BULGARIA

MACEDONIA

TURKEY

TASMANIA
(Australia)

NEW ZEALAND

Some countries in Europe are
crowded together. In this circle,
we have made these countries
bigger so that you can see
them more easily.

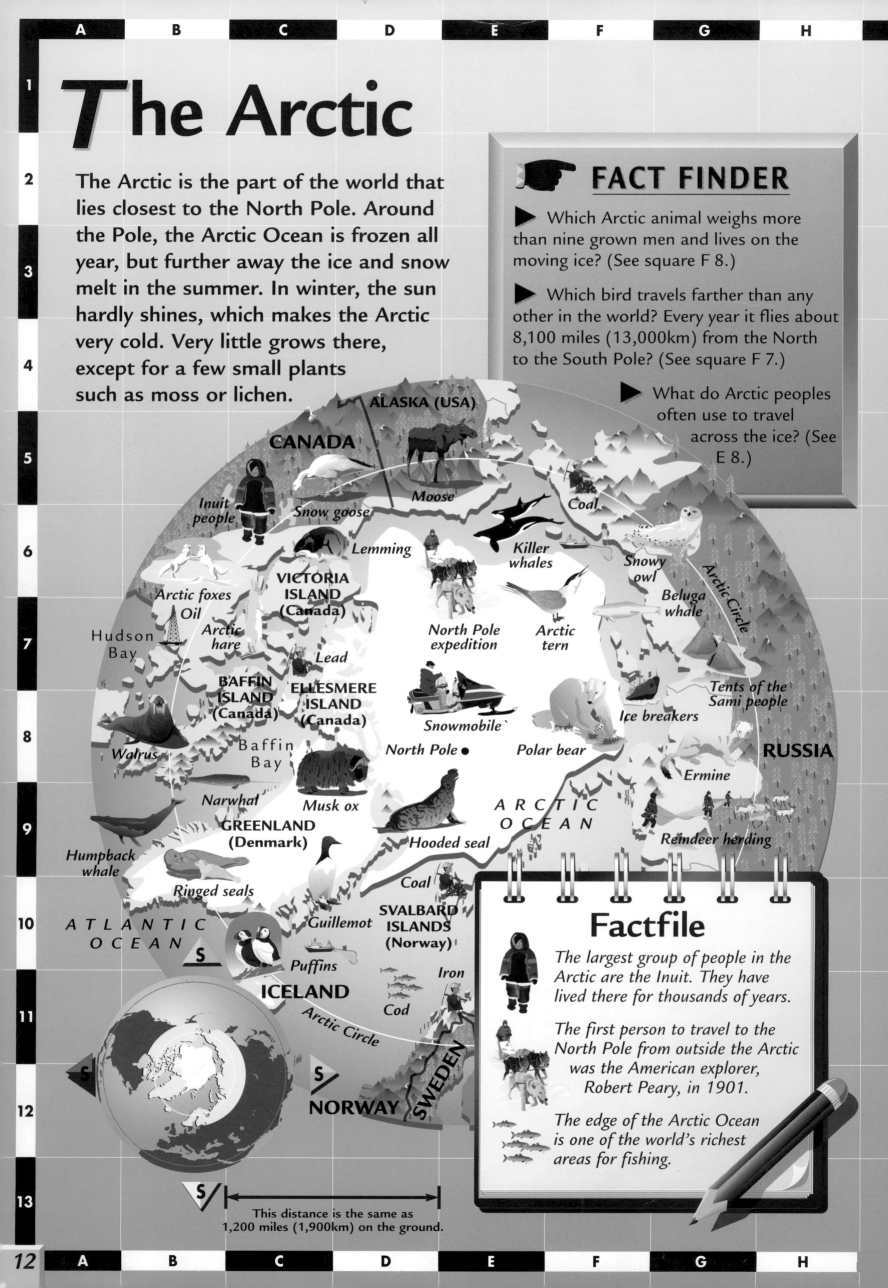

The Arctic

The Arctic is the part of the world that lies closest to the North Pole. Around the Pole, the Arctic Ocean is frozen all year, but further away the ice and snow melt in the summer. In winter, the sun hardly shines, which makes the Arctic very cold. Very little grows there, except for a few small plants such as moss or lichen.

FACT FINDER

► Which Arctic animal weighs more than nine grown men and lives on the moving ice? (See square F 8.)

► Which bird travels farther than any other in the world? Every year it flies about 8,100 miles (13,000km) from the North to the South Pole? (See square F 7.)

► What do Arctic peoples often use to travel across the ice? (See E 8.)

ALASKA (USA)

CANADA

Inuit people

Snow goose

Moose

Coal

Killer whales

Lemming

Snowy owl

VICTORIA ISLAND (Canada)

Arctic foxes

Oil

Arctic hare

North Pole expedition

Arctic tern

Beluga whale

Arctic Circle

Hudson Bay

Lead

BAFFIN ISLAND (Canada)

ELLESMERE ISLAND (Canada)

Tents of the Sami people

Snowmobile

Ice breakers

Walrus

Baffin Bay

North Pole ●

Polar bear

RUSSIA

Ermine

Narwhal

Musk ox

A R C T I C   O C E A N

Humpback whale

GREENLAND (Denmark)

Hooded seal

Reindeer herding

Ringed seals

Coal

A T L A N T I C   O C E A N

Guillemot

SVALBARD ISLANDS (Norway)

S

Puffins

Iron

ICELAND

Cod

Arctic Circle

S

SWEDEN

S

NORWAY

S

This distance is the same as 1,200 miles (1,900km) on the ground.

Factfile

The largest group of people in the Arctic are the Inuit. They have lived there for thousands of years.

The first person to travel to the North Pole from outside the Arctic was the American explorer, Robert Peary, in 1901.

The edge of the Arctic Ocean is one of the world's richest areas for fishing.

Antarctica

Antarctica is an enormous ice-covered continent near the South Pole. It is the coldest and windiest place on Earth. Few animals live around the pole but there are seals and birds on the coast, and plants and fish in the sea. The only people living in Antarctica are scientists. They stay on research stations to study the land and its wildlife.

Factfile

In 1911, Roald Amundsen, a Norwegian explorer, became the first person to reach the South Pole.

Up to 30,000 tourists a year cruise the waters around Antarctica to see the land and its wildlife.

Antarctica has many icebergs. The largest one ever found was over twice the size of the state of Delaware.

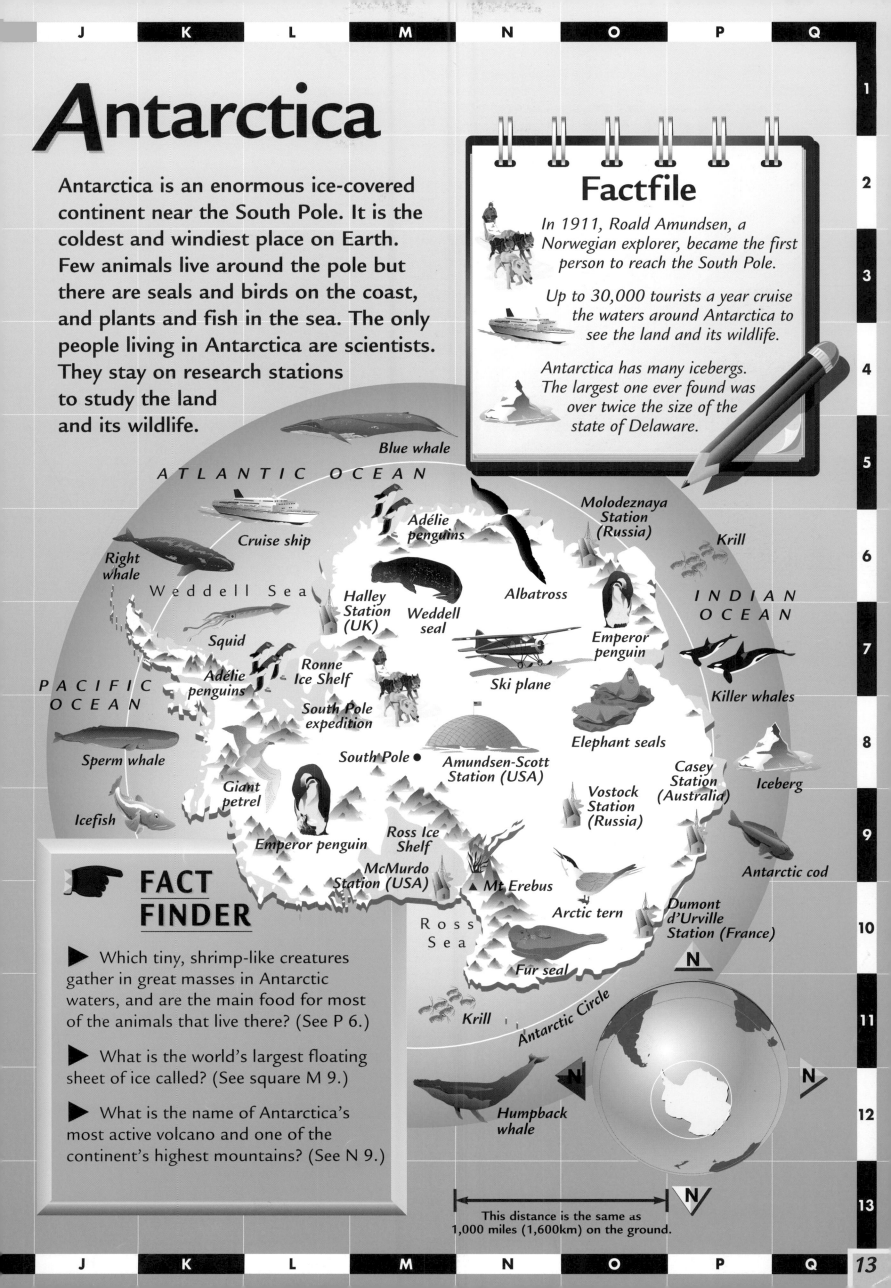

ATLANTIC OCEAN — Blue whale — Cruise ship — Adélie penguins — Right whale — Weddell Sea — Halley Station (UK) — Weddell seal — Squid — Albatross — Molodeznaya Station (Russia) — Krill — INDIAN OCEAN — Emperor penguin — Killer whales — Adélie penguins — Ronne Ice Shelf — South Pole expedition — Ski plane — PACIFIC OCEAN — Sperm whale — South Pole — Amundsen-Scott Station (USA) — Elephant seals — Casey Station (Australia) — Iceberg — Icefish — Giant petrel — Emperor penguin — Ross Ice Shelf — Vostock Station (Russia) — Antarctic cod — McMurdo Station (USA) — Mt Erebus — Arctic tern — Dumont d'Urville Station (France) — Ross Sea — Fur seal — Krill — Antarctic Circle — Humpback whale

FACT FINDER

▶ Which tiny, shrimp-like creatures gather in great masses in Antarctic waters, and are the main food for most of the animals that live there? (See P 6.)

▶ What is the world's largest floating sheet of ice called? (See square M 9.)

▶ What is the name of Antarctica's most active volcano and one of the continent's highest mountains? (See N 9.)

This distance is the same as 1,000 miles (1,600km) on the ground.

1

Canada

2

Canada is the second biggest country in the world
after Russia. Large parts of it are cold and empty.
In the north, there are huge pine forests and the
weather is often freezing. Most people live in
the south where it is warmer. Canada produces
oil and mines coal, silver, gold and copper.
It has good farmland, where farmers grow
enormous fields of wheat. It also has
large factories, mostly in the east,
that make and sell goods, such as
cars, trucks and trains.

A R C T I C   O C E A N

Arctic tern

Ice breakers

Parry Islands

Killer whales

Banks Island

Canadian Royal Mounted Police

Musk ox

Victoria Island

Salmon

ALASKA

YUKON TERRITORY

Oil

Husky dogs

Great Bear Lake

Silver

Arctic foxes

N O R T H W E S T

Mt Logan

River Yukon

Tourism

River Mackenzie

Wolf

Arctic hare

Gold

Silver

Mountain goat

Gas

Great Slave Lake

Oil

Indian carvings

PACIFIC OCEAN

Bald eagle

R O C K Y   M O U N T A I N S

Brown bear

Black bear

Herring

Gas

ALBERTA

Tourism

Forestry

Ice hockey

Forestry

Grizzly bear

Coal

SASKATCHEWAN

BRITISH COLUMBIA

Edmonton

Oil

Apples

Wheat

Buffalo

Vancouver

Barley

Oil

Wheat

Skiing

Pronghorn antelope

Wheat

FACT FINDER

► Which game is played using a
puck and stick on a large ice rink, and
is the country's most popular sport?
(See square F 9.)

► Which large animal once roamed
in huge herds over Canada's grasslands
but now lives mostly in national parks?
(See square H 10.)

► Canada has two main languages,
English and French. In which province,
or district, would you find most of the
French speakers? (See square N 9.)

UNITED STATES OF AMERICA

This distance is the same as
500 miles (800km) on the ground.

Ellesmere Island

GREENLAND (Denmark)

Queen Elizabeth Islands

Lemming

Walrus

Beluga whale

Hooded seal

Narwhal

Prince of Wales Island

Inuit people

Baffin Island

Snowy owl

Arctic Circle

Polar bear

Snowmobile

TERRITORIES

Starfish

Humpback whale

ATLANTIC OCEAN

Canada geese

Ice breakers

Lynx

Iron

Puffins

Right whale

Moose

H u d s o n B a y

Mink

Snow goose

Float plane

NEWFOUNDLAND

Cod

MANITOBA

River Nelson

QUEBEC

Iron

Forestry

Copper

Beaver

Ermine

Forestry

Maple syrup

Making paper

Tourism

ONTARIO

Red squirrel

Gold

Tourist bus

Copper

Dairy cattle

Oil

Château Frontenac

NEW BRUNSWICK

Road train

Racoon

Iron

Potatoes

NOVA SCOTIA

Winnipeg

Apples

Beef cattle

Iron

Lake Superior

Coal

PRINCE EDWARD ISLAND

Blue whale

CN Tower

Montreal

Lake Huron

Ottawa

Car building

Toronto

Lake Ontario

Pigs

Lake Michigan

Lake Erie

Niagara Falls

Lobster

River St Lawrence

Gulf of St Lawrence

Factfile

Forests cover more than one-third of Canada. The trees are cut down by lumberjacks and made into timber and paper.

Canada is famous for its sweet maple syrup. It is made in the spring from the sticky sap of sugar maple trees.

In Canada no one is far from water. The country has over one million lakes. Lake Superior, on the border between Canada and the United States, is the largest freshwater lake in the world.

The United States

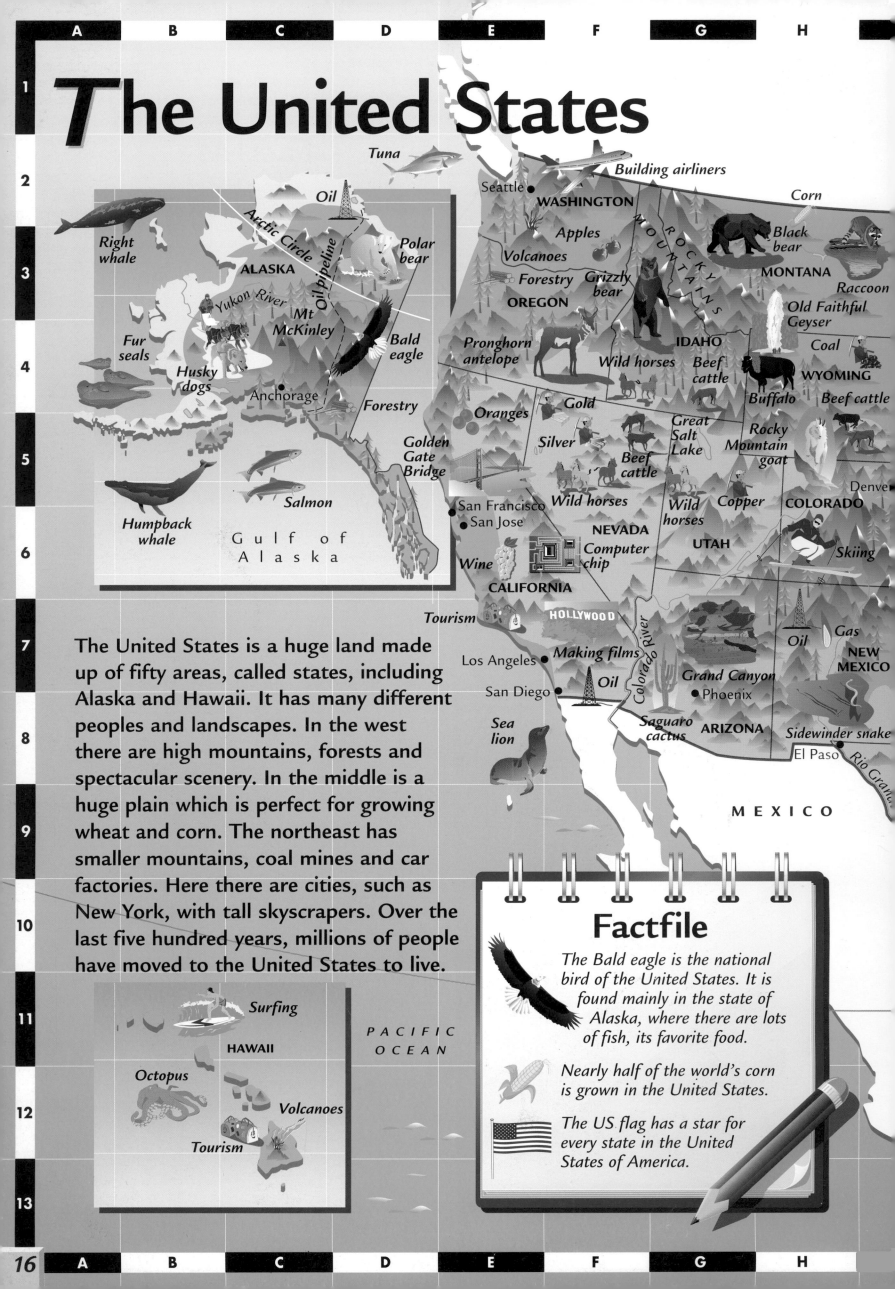

Tuna

Building airliners

Corn

Seattle
WASHINGTON
Apples
Volcanoes
ROCKY MOUNTAINS
Black bear
Raccoon
MONTANA

Oil
Arctic Circle
Oil pipeline
Polar bear
Right whale
ALASKA
Yukon River
Mt McKinley
Bald eagle
Fur seals
Husky dogs
Anchorage
Forestry
Golden Gate Bridge

Forestry
Grizzly bear
OREGON
Pronghorn antelope
Wild horses
IDAHO
Beef cattle
Old Faithful Geyser
Coal
WYOMING
Buffalo
Beef cattle

Oranges
Gold
Silver
Beef cattle
Wild horses
Great Salt Lake
Rocky Mountain goat
Copper
COLORADO
Denver

Humpback whale
Salmon
Gulf of Alaska
San Francisco
San Jose
Wine
CALIFORNIA
Computer chip
NEVADA
Wild horses
UTAH
Skiing

Tourism
HOLLYWOOD
Making films
Los Angeles
San Diego
Oil
Sea lion
Colorado River
Grand Canyon
Phoenix
Saguaro cactus
ARIZONA
El Paso
Oil
Gas
NEW MEXICO
Sidewinder snake
Rio Grande

MEXICO

The United States is a huge land made up of fifty areas, called states, including Alaska and Hawaii. It has many different peoples and landscapes. In the west there are high mountains, forests and spectacular scenery. In the middle is a huge plain which is perfect for growing wheat and corn. The northeast has smaller mountains, coal mines and car factories. Here there are cities, such as New York, with tall skyscrapers. Over the last five hundred years, millions of people have moved to the United States to live.

Surfing
PACIFIC OCEAN
HAWAII
Octopus
Volcanoes
Tourism

Factfile

The Bald eagle is the national bird of the United States. It is found mainly in the state of Alaska, where there are lots of fish, its favorite food.

Nearly half of the world's corn is grown in the United States.

The US flag has a star for every state in the United States of America.

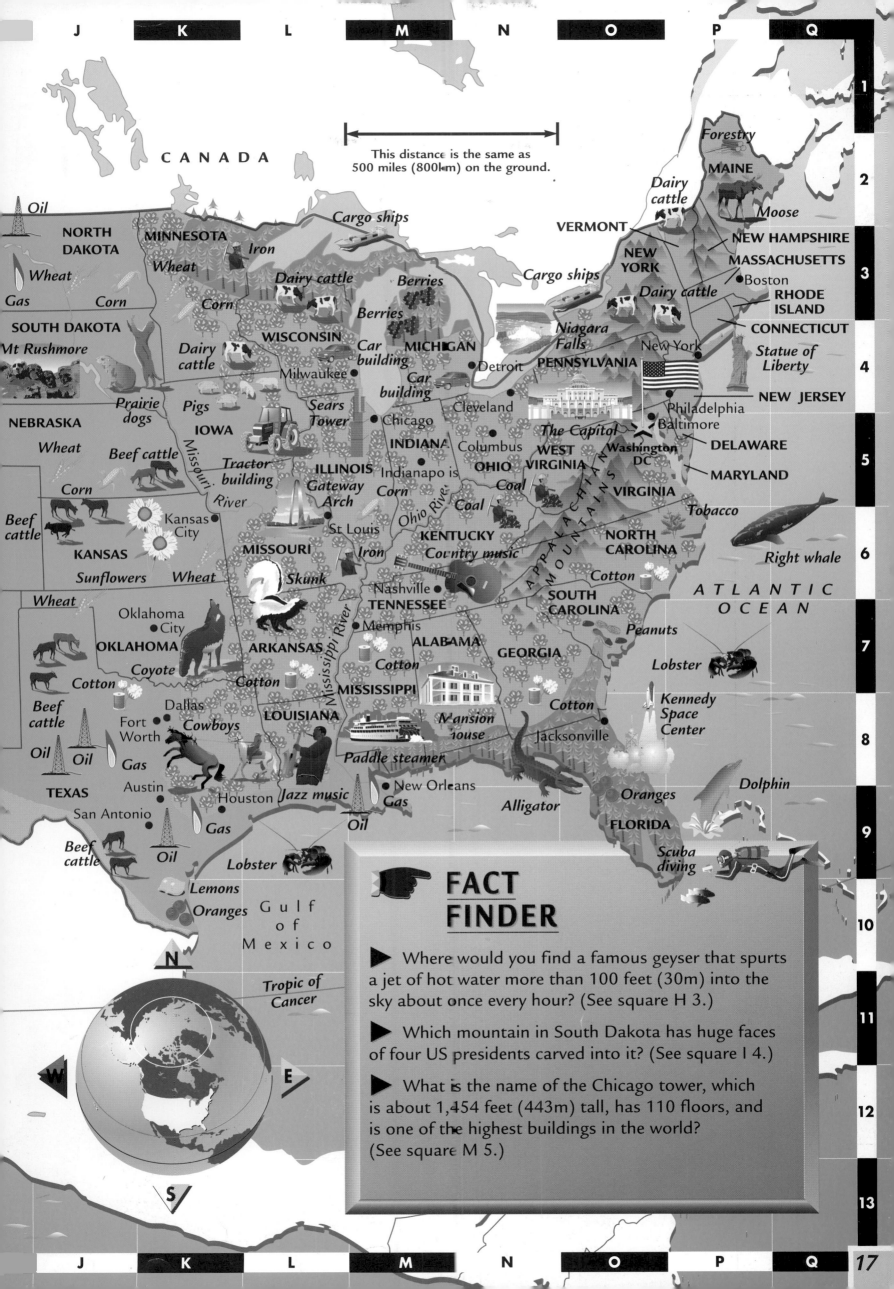

J K L M N O P Q

1 2 3 4 5 6 7 8 9 10 11 12 13

CANADA

This distance is the same as 500 miles (800km) on the ground.

Oil
NORTH DAKOTA
Wheat
Gas
Corn
SOUTH DAKOTA
Mt Rushmore
NEBRASKA
Wheat
Beef cattle
Corn
Beef cattle
KANSAS
Sunflowers
Wheat
Wheat
Oklahoma City
OKLAHOMA
Coyote
Cotton
Beef cattle
Oil
Oil
Gas
Austin
TEXAS
San Antonio
Dallas
Fort Worth
Cowboys
Houston
Gas
Beef cattle
Oil
Lobster
Lemons
Oranges
Gulf of Mexico
Tropic of Cancer

MINNESOTA
Wheat
Iron
Corn
Dairy cattle
WISCONSIN
Dairy cattle
Milwaukee
Pigs
IOWA
Prairie dogs
Tractor building
ILLINOIS
Gateway Arch
Sears Tower
Chicago
St Louis
MISSOURI
Iron
Skunk
Nashville
TENNESSEE
Memphis
ARKANSAS
Cotton
Cotton
MISSISSIPPI
LOUISIANA
Paddle steamer
Mansion house
New Orleans
Gas
Oil
Jazz music
Missouri River
Mississippi River

Cargo ships
Berries
Berries
Car building
MICHIGAN
Car building
Detroit
Cleveland
INDIANA
Columbus
Indianapolis
OHIO
Corn
Ohio River
Coal
KENTUCKY
Country music
Cotton
ALABAMA
GEORGIA
Cotton
Jacksonville

Cargo ships
VERMONT
NEW YORK
Niagara Falls
New York
PENNSYLVANIA
The Capitol
Washington DC
WEST VIRGINIA
Coal
Coal
VIRGINIA
Tobacco
NORTH CAROLINA
Cotton
SOUTH CAROLINA
Peanuts
Lobster
Kennedy Space Center
Oranges
Alligator
FLORIDA
Scuba diving
Dolphin

Forestry
MAINE
Dairy cattle
Moose
NEW HAMPSHIRE
MASSACHUSETTS
Boston
RHODE ISLAND
CONNECTICUT
Dairy cattle
Statue of Liberty
NEW JERSEY
Philadelphia
Baltimore
DELAWARE
MARYLAND
Right whale
ATLANTIC OCEAN

N
W
E
S

FACT FINDER

► Where would you find a famous geyser that spurts a jet of hot water more than 100 feet (30m) into the sky about once every hour? (See square H 3.)

► Which mountain in South Dakota has huge faces of four US presidents carved into it? (See square I 4.)

► What is the name of the Chicago tower, which is about 1,454 feet (443m) tall, has 110 floors, and is one of the highest buildings in the world? (See square M 5.)

J K L M N O P Q

17

Central America and the Caribbean

A B C D E F G H

1
2
3
4
5
6
7
8
9
10
11
12
13

18

Saguaro cactus

BAJA CALIFORNIA

Sea lion

Elephant seals

Blue whale

P A C I F I C
O C E A N

Humpback whale

Polka dot
grouper fish

SIERRA MADRE

Beef
cattle

Cotton

Silver

Rice

Coyote

Beef
cattle

MEXICO

Spectacled
bear

Tobacco

Tourism

Forestry

Iron

Tourism

Acapulco

N

W

E

S

**UNITED STATES
OF AMERICA**

Rio Grande

Armadillo

Cotton

G u l f   o f   M e x i c o

Lobster

Anchovies

Grapefruit

Lemons

Oranges

Corn

Corn

Shrimp

Oil

Mexico City

Sugar
cane

Corn

Corn

Corn

Corn

Coffee

Scarlet
macaw

Spider
monkey

Chichén
Itzá

Tourism

Belmopan

BELIZE

GUATEMALA

Guatemala City

San Salvador

EL SALVADOR

Coffee

Tegucig-
alpa

Managua

Factfile

Mexico is one of the world's
biggest producers of silver.

The Caribbean Islands are some
of the world's most popular
holiday places. Cruise ships
carry passengers from one
island to another.

Honduras is one of the world's
largest producers of bananas.
The fruit is green when it is
picked, but ripens as it is
shipped across the world.

Teardrop
butterfly fish

Swordfish

Clown fish

Sea horses

Sperm whale

This distance is the same as
430 miles (700km) on the ground.

A B C D E F G H

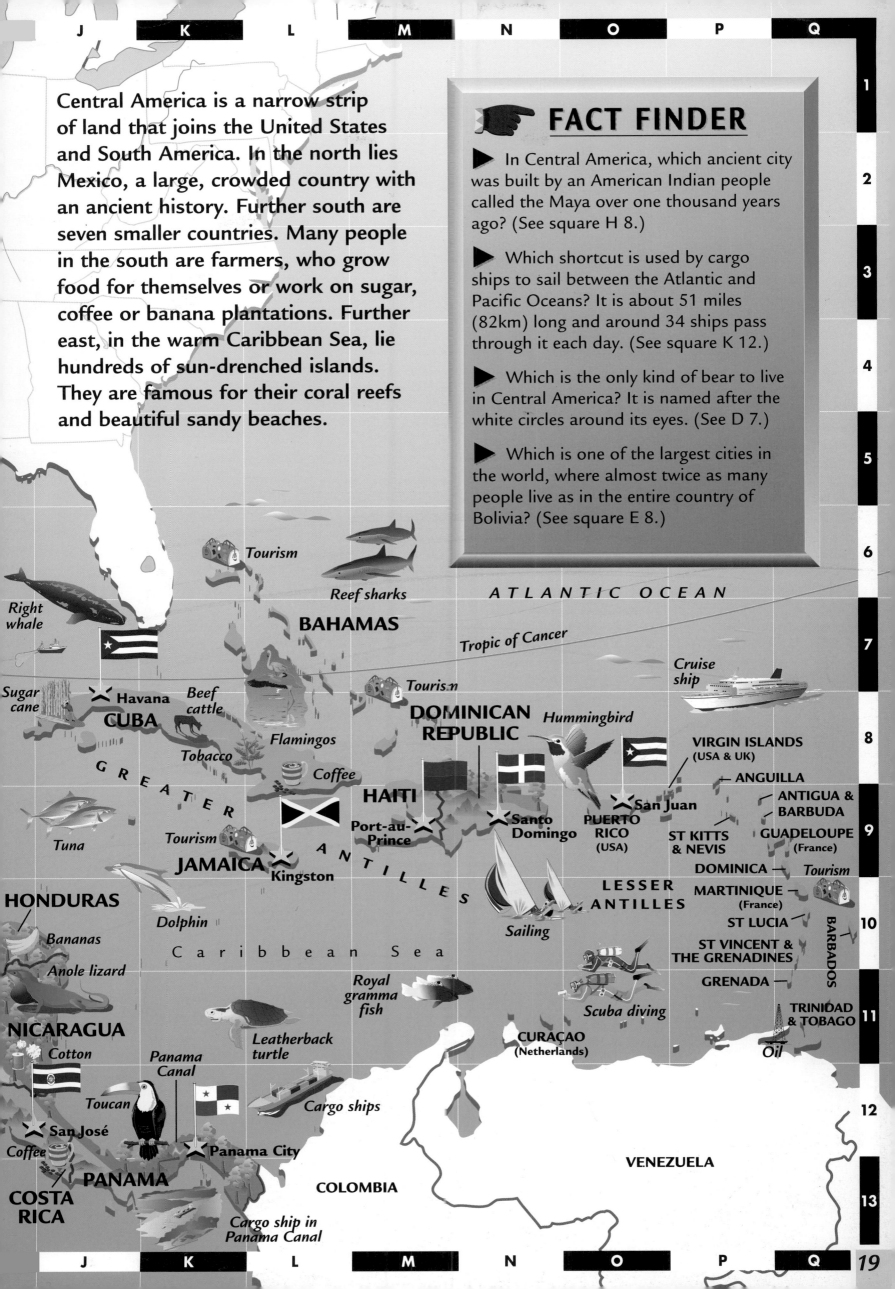

Central America is a narrow strip of land that joins the United States and South America. In the north lies Mexico, a large, crowded country with an ancient history. Further south are seven smaller countries. Many people in the south are farmers, who grow food for themselves or work on sugar, coffee or banana plantations. Further east, in the warm Caribbean Sea, lie hundreds of sun-drenched islands. They are famous for their coral reefs and beautiful sandy beaches.

👉 FACT FINDER

► In Central America, which ancient city was built by an American Indian people called the Maya over one thousand years ago? (See square H 8.)

► Which shortcut is used by cargo ships to sail between the Atlantic and Pacific Oceans? It is about 51 miles (82km) long and around 34 ships pass through it each day. (See square K 12.)

► Which is the only kind of bear to live in Central America? It is named after the white circles around its eyes. (See D 7.)

► Which is one of the largest cities in the world, where almost twice as many people live as in the entire country of Bolivia? (See square E 8.)

Tourism

Reef sharks

ATLANTIC OCEAN

Right whale

Sugar cane

Havana

CUBA

Beef cattle

Tobacco

BAHAMAS

Tropic of Cancer

Cruise ship

Tourism

DOMINICAN REPUBLIC

Hummingbird

VIRGIN ISLANDS (USA & UK)

ANGUILLA

Flamingos

Coffee

San Juan

ANTIGUA & BARBUDA

Tuna

GREATER

HAITI

PUERTO RICO (USA)

ST KITTS & NEVIS

GUADELOUPE (France)

Tourism

Port-au-Prince

Santo Domingo

DOMINICA

Tourism

JAMAICA

ANTILLES

LESSER ANTILLES

MARTINIQUE (France)

Kingston

ST LUCIA

HONDURAS

Dolphin

Sailing

ST VINCENT & THE GRENADINES

BARBADOS

Bananas

Caribbean Sea

GRENADA

Anole lizard

Royal gramma fish

Scuba diving

TRINIDAD & TOBAGO

NICARAGUA

Leatherback turtle

CURAÇAO (Netherlands)

Oil

Cotton

Panama Canal

Cargo ships

Toucan

San José

Panama City

VENEZUELA

Coffee

PANAMA

COLOMBIA

COSTA RICA

Cargo ship in Panama Canal

South America

20

The continent of South America stretches from the warm Caribbean Sea to the stormy waters around Cape Horn. South America is warm all year, except in the far south and in the high Andes Mountains. In the north, the great River Amazon flows through tropical rainforest. Further south, there are flat plains where millions of cattle graze. Most South Americans live in cities on the coast. In the country, the farmers grow bananas, coffee beans and corn.

Caribbean Sea

Cargo ships

Royal gramma fish

Caracas
VENEZUELA
Oil
Oil
Oil

Cayenne
FRENCH GUIANA (France)

Paramaribo
SURINAME
Rice

Georgetown
GUYANA
Rice

Tourism
Bananas
Gold
Cow tree
Making clothes
River Orinoco
Diamonds
Gold

Angel Falls
Gold

Equator
Shrimp

Crocodile
Piranha fish
Toucan
Oil

Emerald tree boa
River Amazon
Amazon rainforest

Dug-out canoes
Stilt house

Emeralds
Bogotá
COLOMBIA
Coffee
Coffee

Cali
Quito
ECUADOR
Coffee
Oil
Bananas
Herring

Sperm whale

Tapir
Umbrella bird
Arrow-poison frog
Llama
Cotton
Oil
Coffee
Copper
Lima
PERU
Sugar cane
Gold
Lake Titicaca
Cotton

Sloth
Jaguar
Vampire bat
BRAZIL
Corn
Gold
Iron
Gold
Oil
Gold
Wheat
Cattle ranching

Sugar cane
BOLIVIA
La Paz
Gas
Cotton
Potatoes
Copper
Tin
Corn
Cotton

Diamonds
Rainforest clearing
River São Francisco
Brasília
Corn
Iron
Rice
Oranges
Tourism
Iron
Cotton
Coffee

Tobacco
Sugar cane
Cotton
Gold
Oil
Recife
Cargo ships
Shrimp
Lobster

Carnival
Rio de Janeiro

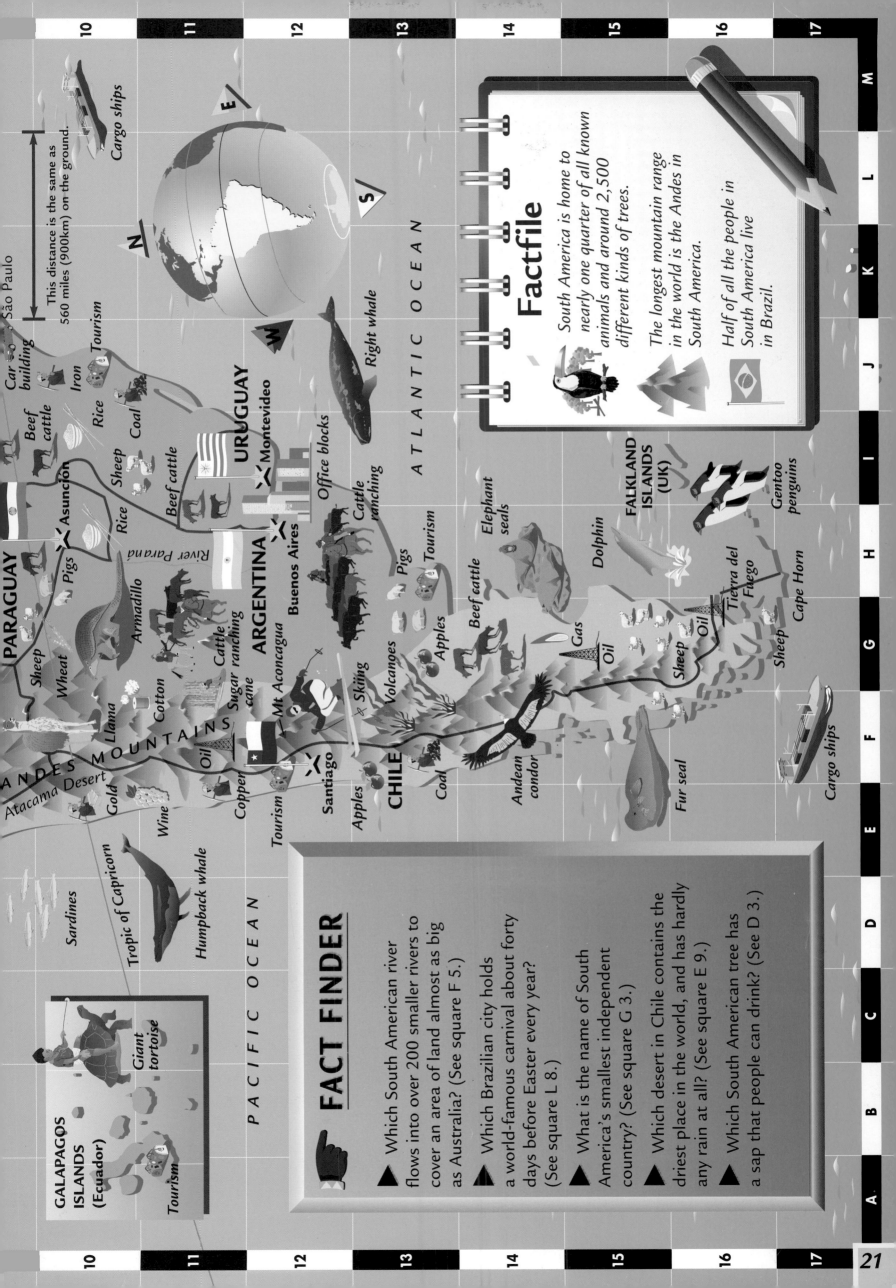

This distance is the same as 560 miles (900km) on the ground.

Cargo ships

Cargo shi... São Paulo
building
Iron Tourism
Beef cattle
Rice
Sheep
Coal
Rice
Beef cattle

PARAGUAY

Sheep
Wheat
Pigs
Llama
Armadillo
Cotton
Asunción
River Paraná
Sugar cane
Cattle ranching

Oil
Copper
Tourism
Gold
Wine
Atacama Desert

ANDES MOUNTAINS

Mt Aconcagua
Skiing
Volcanoes
Apples

CHILE
Santiago
Apples
Coal

Andean condor

N
S
W
E

URUGUAY
Montevideo

ARGENTINA
Buenos Aires

Office blocks
Cattle ranching

Pigs
Tourism
Apples
Beef cattle
Elephant seals

Right whale

ATLANTIC OCEAN

Gas
Oil

Dolphin

FALKLAND ISLANDS (UK)

Sheep
Oil
Tierra del Fuego
Cape Horn
Sheep
Gentoo penguins

Fur seal

PACIFIC OCEAN

Sardines
Tropic of Capricorn
Humpback whale

GALAPAGOS ISLANDS (Ecuador)

Giant tortoise
Tourism

Cargo ships

Factfile

South America is home to nearly one quarter of all known animals and around 2,500 different kinds of trees.

The longest mountain range in the world is the Andes in South America.

Half of all the people in South America live in Brazil.

☛ # FACT FINDER

▲ Which South American river flows into over 200 smaller rivers to cover an area of land almost as big as Australia? (See square F 5.)

▲ Which Brazilian city holds a world-famous carnival about forty days before Easter every year? (See square L 8.)

▲ What is the name of South America's smallest independent country? (See square G 3.)

▲ Which desert in Chile contains the driest place in the world, and has hardly any rain at all? (See square E 9.)

▲ Which South American tree has a sap that people can drink? (See D 3.)

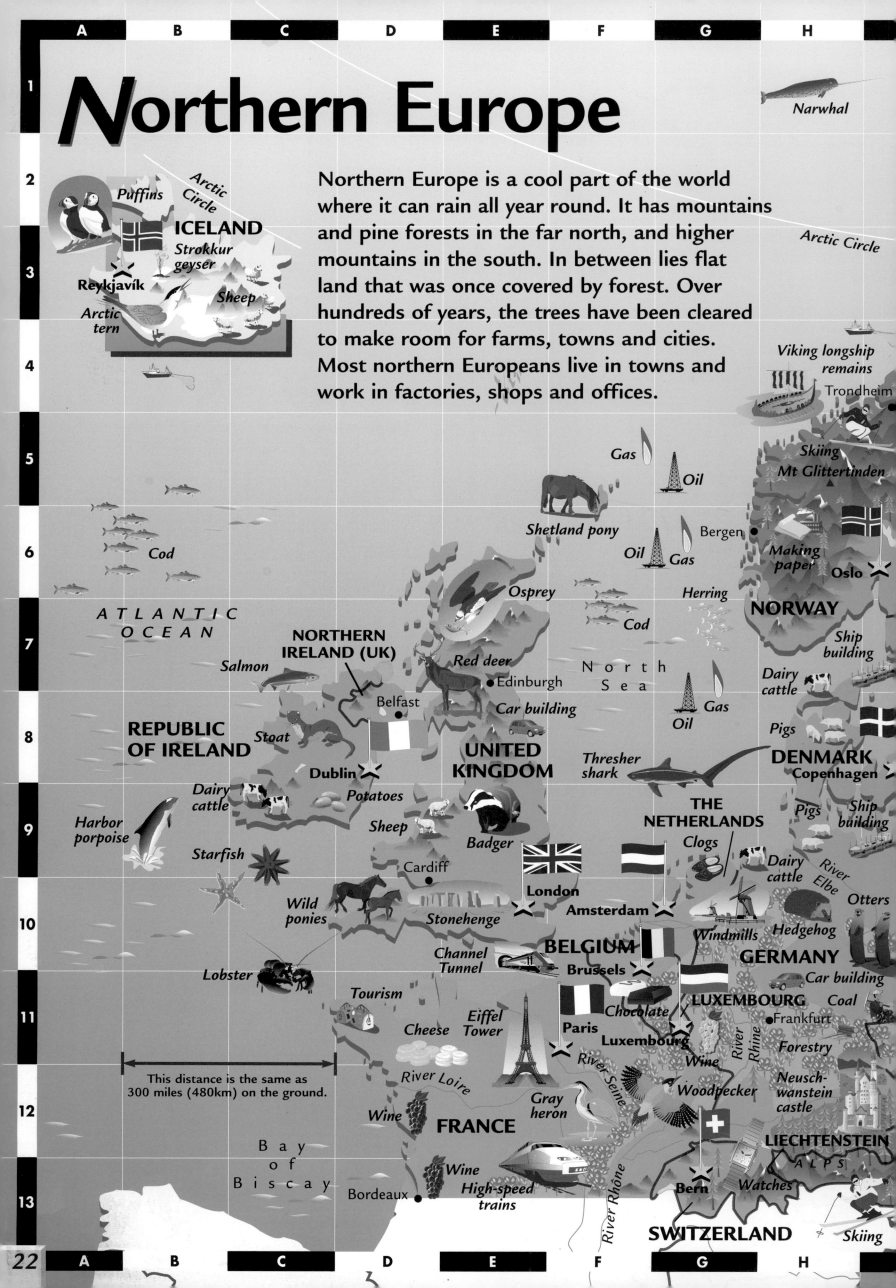

Northern Europe

Narwhal

Northern Europe is a cool part of the world where it can rain all year round. It has mountains and pine forests in the far north, and higher mountains in the south. In between lies flat land that was once covered by forest. Over hundreds of years, the trees have been cleared to make room for farms, towns and cities. Most northern Europeans live in towns and work in factories, shops and offices.

Arctic Circle

Puffins

Arctic Circle

ICELAND

Strokkur geyser

Reykjavík

Arctic tern

Sheep

Viking longship remains

Trondheim

Skiing
Mt Glittertinden

Gas

Oil

Shetland pony

Bergen

Making paper

Oslo

Oil   Gas

Herring

NORWAY

Osprey

Cod

Ship building

A T L A N T I C
O C E A N

Cod

N o r t h
S e a

Dairy cattle

NORTHERN IRELAND (UK)

Salmon

Red deer

Edinburgh

Gas

Car building

Oil

Pigs

Belfast

Thresher shark

DENMARK
Copenhagen

REPUBLIC OF IRELAND

Stoat

UNITED KINGDOM

Pigs

Ship building

Dublin

Potatoes

THE NETHERLANDS

Dairy cattle

Harbor porpoise

Dairy cattle

Sheep

Clogs

Dairy cattle

River Elbe

Badger

Starfish

Otters

Cardiff

London

Windmills

Hedgehog

Wild ponies

Stonehenge

Amsterdam

GERMANY

Lobster

Channel Tunnel

BELGIUM

Brussels

Car building

LUXEMBOURG   Coal

Tourism

Chocolate

Frankfurt

Cheese

Eiffel Tower

Paris

Luxembourg

River Rhine

Forestry

Wine

River Seine

Wine

Neuschwanstein castle

This distance is the same as 300 miles (480km) on the ground.

River Loire

Gray heron

Woodpecker

B a y
o f
B i s c a y

Wine

FRANCE

LIECHTENSTEIN

A L P S

Watches

Wine

High-speed trains

Bern

Bordeaux

Skiing

SWITZERLAND

Norwegian
Sea

L a p l a n d

Reindeer

Sami people

Iron

Forestry

K J Ø L E N   M O U N T A I N S

Cross-country skiing

Forestry

Lynx

FINLAND

Forestry

Forestry

*Making
paper*

SWEDEN

Making paper

Salmon

Herring

Fox

Helsinki

Stockholm

*Ice
breakers*

Tallinn

Pigs

ESTONIA

Car building

*Building
trains*

Göteborg

*Dairy
cattle*

Riga

LATVIA

B a l t i c
S e a

LITHUANIA

• Malmö

Vilnius

Ship building

Kaliningrad
(Russia)

Ship building

Dairy cattle

Potatoes

Chaffinch

Red squirrel

Berlin

Warsaw

Wild boar

POLAND

Coal

Wolf

Prague

Chamois

**CZECH
REPUBLIC**

UKRAINE

SLOVAKIA

Vienna

River Danube

Bratislava

AUSTRIA

*Peregrine
falcon*

*Parliament
building*

Budapest

ROMANIA

HUNGARY

Wild horses

RUSSIA

N

W   E

S

BELARUS

FACT FINDER

► Which tunnel in northern Europe is about 31 miles (50km) long, was opened in 1994 and is often called the "Chunnel"? (See square E 10.)

► In which country could you see a long ship on display, which was built by the Viking people hundreds of years ago? (See square H 4.)

► Which famous European tower is about 984 feet (320m) high and has 1,652 steps that take you to the top? (See square E 11.)

► Which stone monument in England was built around 3,500 years ago, but nobody knows what it was used for? (See square E 10.)

Factfile

There are twice as many pigs in Denmark as people. Two out of three pigs are exported as Danish bacon.

France is visited by more tourists each year than any other country in the world.

Finland produces enough paper to make 5 million comics every day.

Southern Europe

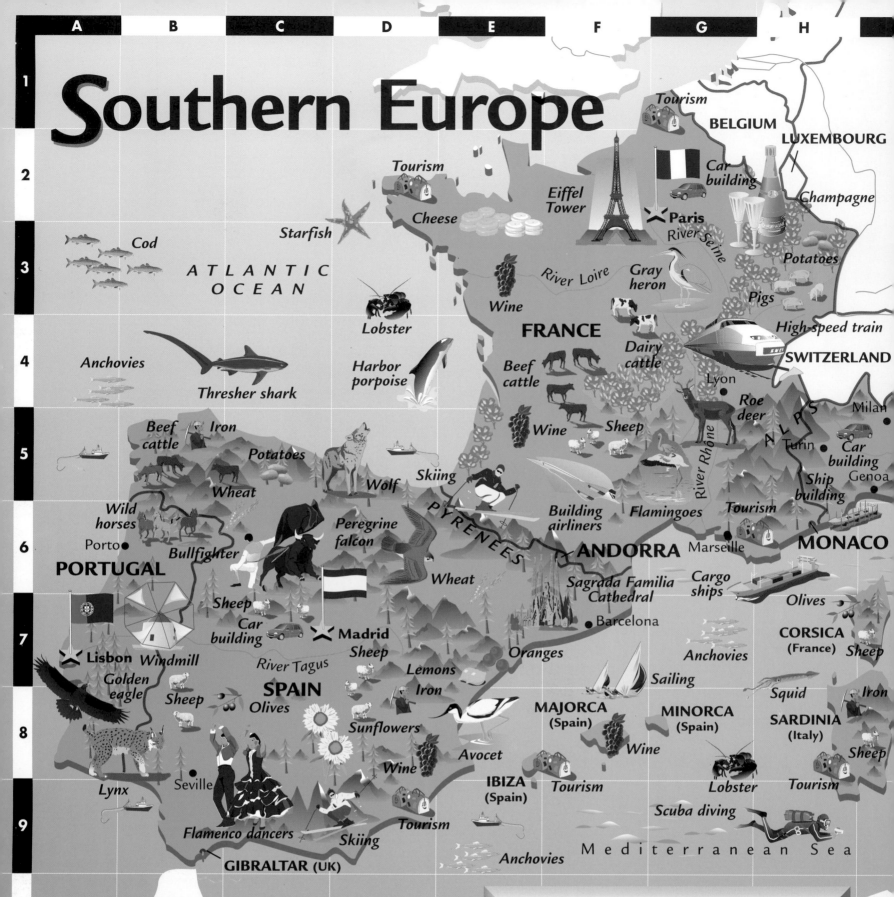

BELGIUM

LUXEMBOURG

Tourism

Cheese

Eiffel Tower

Car building

Champagne

Paris

River Seine

Potatoes

River Loire

FRANCE

Gray heron

Pigs

High-speed train

Cod

Starfish

ATLANTIC OCEAN

Wine

SWITZERLAND

Lobster

Dairy cattle

Lyon

Roe deer

Milan

Anchovies

Harbor porpoise

Beef cattle

Turin

Car building

Thresher shark

Wine

Sheep

River Rhône

Genoa

Beef cattle

Iron

Skiing

Ship building

Potatoes

Building airliners

Flamingoes

Tourism

MONACO

Wheat

Wild horses

Wolf

PYRENEES

ANDORRA

Marseille

Porto

Bullfighter

Peregrine falcon

Sagrada Familia Cathedral

Cargo ships

Olives

PORTUGAL

Wheat

Barcelona

CORSICA (France)

Sheep

Sheep

Car building

Madrid

Oranges

Anchovies

Lisbon

Windmill

Sheep

Sailing

Squid

Iron

Golden eagle

River Tagus

Lemons

Iron

MAJORCA (Spain)

MINORCA (Spain)

SARDINIA (Italy)

Sheep

Olives

SPAIN

Sunflowers

Wine

Lynx

Avocet

Wine

Lobster

Tourism

Seville

IBIZA (Spain)

Tourism

Scuba diving

Flamenco dancers

Skiing

Tourism

Anchovies

Mediterranean Sea

GIBRALTAR (UK)

Southern Europe is warm, sunny and mainly dry. Large parts of it are covered with mountains and hills, but there is still plenty of good farmland. Many people in southern Europe are farmers. They grow cereals and all kinds of fruit and vegetables. Southern Europe also has many famous ancient buildings and works of art. Each year millions of tourists visit its museums and art galleries.

FACT FINDER

▶ Which Italian bell tower, built over 300 years ago, began to lean before it was even finished? (See square I 6.)

▶ What is the name of the ancient Roman stadium where gladiators once fought with swords and nets? (See J 7.)

▶ Which ancient Greek temple was built to worship the goddess Athene, protector of Athens? (See square N 8.)

POLAND

N

UKRAINE

GERMANY

CZECH REPUBLIC

W **E**

This distance is the same as 250 miles (400km) on the ground.

AUSTRIA

S

Skiing

Potatoes

MOLDOVA

Sheep

Forestry

Wine

HUNGARY

Wolf

Wheat

Chamois

Tobacco

Red squirrel

ROMANIA

Making clothes

Ljubljana

Zagreb

Tractor building

Pizza Tourism

Venice

SLOVENIA

CROATIA

Olives

Sheep

Bucharest

Pelican

River Po

Brown bear

Belgrade

Oil

Ship building

BOSNIA-HERZEGOVINA

Gas

River Danube

B l a c k S e a

Making clothes

SAN MARINO

Sarajevo

FEDERAL REPUBLIC OF YUGOSLAVIA

BULGARIA

Leaning Tower of Pisa

Wild boar

Sofia

Sunflowers

ITALY

Ponte Vecchio, Florence

Dubrovnik

Tractor building

Octopus

TURKEY

Vatican City

Beef cattle

Skopje

Rome

MACEDONIA

Istanbul

The Colosseum

Olives

Tobacco

Naples

Mt Vesuvius

Olives

Tirané

Goats

TURKEY

Sardines

ALBANIA

Tobacco

Tobacco

Swordfish

Wine

Mt Olympus

Tobacco

Wine

GREECE

Coot

Squid

Tourism

Tuna

Wheat

Palermo

Oranges

Octopus

SICILY (Italy)

Lemons

The Parthenon

Wine

Mt Etna

Cargo ships

Athens

Tourism

Oranges

Olives

Tourism

MALTA

Tourism

Factfile

Mount Etna in Sicily is the largest volcano in Europe. It last erupted in 1995.

Ship building

Tuna

Wine

Spain produces more olive oil than any other country. Each year it produces enough olive oil to fill 160 Olympic-sized swimming pools.

Olives

Squid

CRETE (Greece)

Anchovies

Russia and its neighbors

FACT FINDER

▶ Which space center launched the world's first astronaut, Yuri Gagarin, into space in 1961? (See square G 8.)

▶ Which Russian railway line is the longest railway line in the world? It takes seven days to travel along it from one end to the other. (See square J 8.)

This distance is the same as 700 miles (1,100km) on the ground.

Russia stretches across Europe and Asia and is the largest country in the world. Russia and its neighbors used to be called the Soviet Union, but in 1991 the Union split up. Most Russians live in the part of Russia that is in Europe, which has many cities and good farmland. Far away to the north and east is a huge forest called the taiga, where wolves and bears roam.

Factfile

Russia first used this flag in 1699. But when Russia formed the Soviet Union, the flag was replaced. In 1991, the Soviet Union broke up, and Russia began to use the old flag once more.

Russia and its neighbors produce more oil than anywhere else in the world.

Southwest Asia

The southwest corner of Asia is also called the Middle East. Here, thousands of years ago, people first became farmers, then settled close together in towns. Much of the land in southwest Asia is hot, dry desert, which can be hard to farm. Fifty years ago, people found oil under the desert. They used the money they made from the oil to build huge watering systems, so they could grow crops more easily in the poor soil. They also built large cities.

Factfile

Over 5,000 years ago, the first cities in the world grew up in southwest Asia, along the Tigris and Euphrates Rivers.

Three of the world's major religions began in southwest Asia. They are Islam, Judaism and Christianity.

Southwest Asia makes some of the world's most expensive hand-made carpets. Carpet-makers weave and knot wool to make different patterns which can tell you the area the carpet comes from.

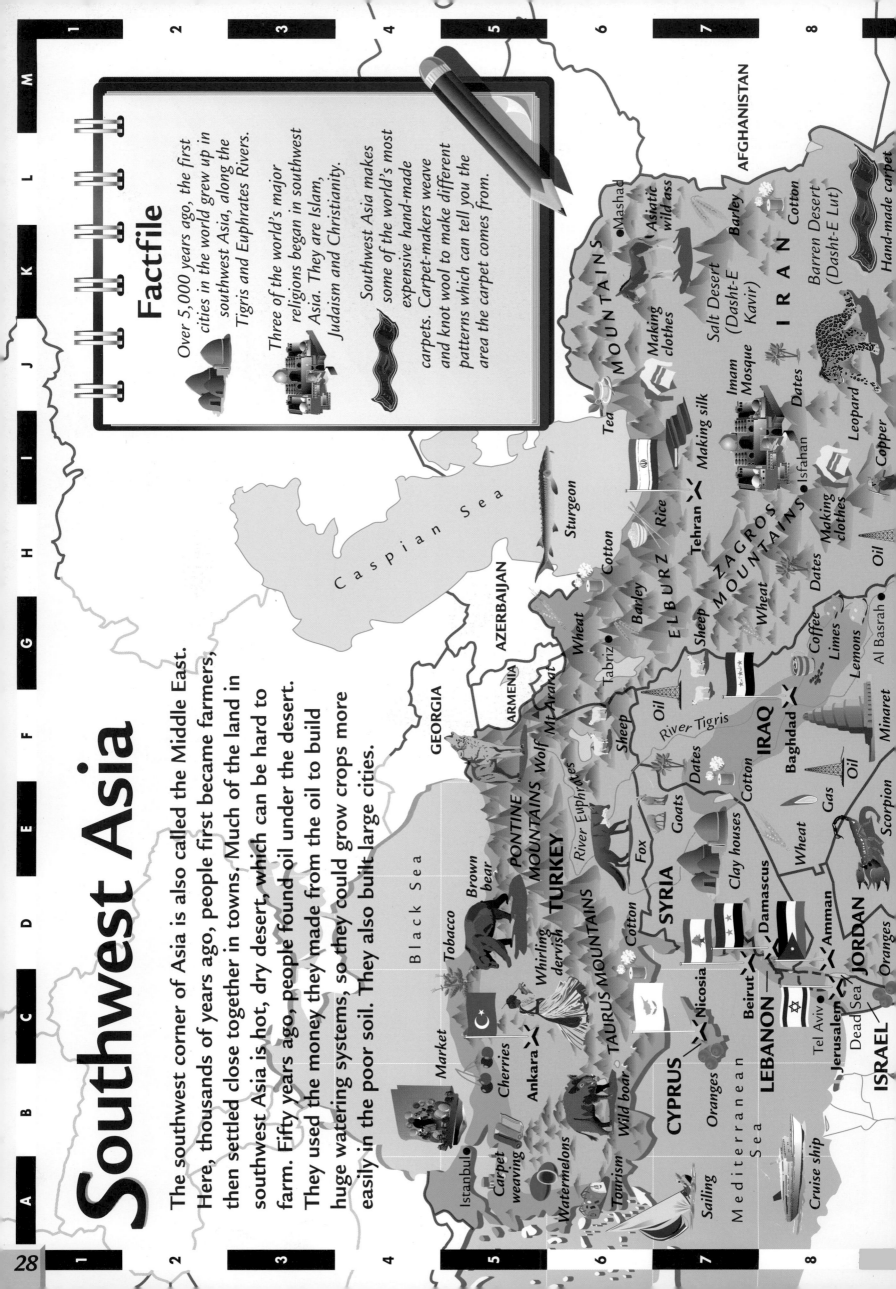

Caspian Sea

Black Sea

Mediterranean Sea

GEORGIA

ARMENIA

AZERBAIJAN

TURKEY

CYPRUS

LEBANON

SYRIA

ISRAEL

JORDAN

IRAQ

IRAN

AFGHANISTAN

PONTINE MOUNTAINS

TAURUS MOUNTAINS

ELBURZ MOUNTAINS

ZAGROS MOUNTAINS

Istanbul
Ankara
Nicosia
Beirut
Tel Aviv
Jerusalem
Damascus
Amman
Baghdad
Tabriz
Tehran
Isfahan
Mashad
Al Basrah

Dead Sea

River Euphrates
River Tigris

Mt Ararat

Barren Desert (Dasht-E Lut)
Salt Desert (Dasht-E Kavir)

Market
Carpet weaving
Watermelons
Tourism
Wild boar
Cherries
Oranges
Sailing
Cruise ship
Oranges
Tobacco
Brown bear
Whirling dervish
Cotton
Clay houses
Cotton
Goats
Fox
Sheep
Dates
Wheat
Gas
Oil
Scorpion
Minaret
Wheat
Coffee
Limes
Lemons
Dates
Sheep
Wheat
Barley
Rice
Oil
Cotton
Sturgeon
Tea
Making silk
Making clothes
Imam Mosque
Dates
Making clothes
Leopard
Copper
Asiatic wild ass
Barley
Cotton
Hand-made carpet
Wolf

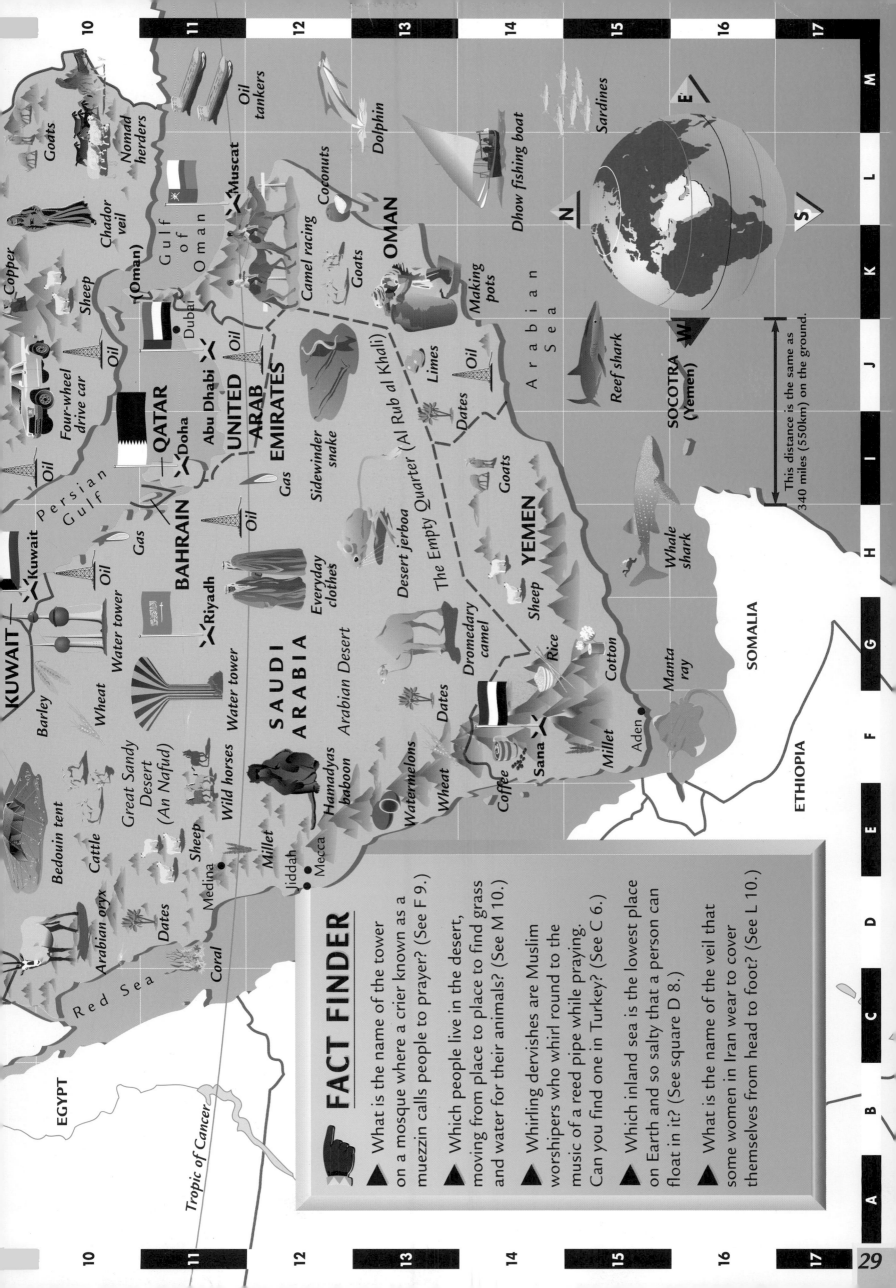

FACT FINDER

▲ What is the name of the tower on a mosque where a crier known as a muezzin calls people to prayer? (See F 9.)

▲ Which people live in the desert, moving from place to place to find grass and water for their animals? (See M 10.)

▲ Whirling dervishes are Muslim worshipers who whirl round to the music of a reed pipe while praying. Can you find one in Turkey? (See C 6.)

▲ Which inland sea is the lowest place on Earth and so salty that a person can float in it? (See square D 8.)

▲ What is the name of the veil that some women in Iran wear to cover themselves from head to foot? (See L 10.)

EGYPT

Tropic of Cancer

Red Sea

Coral

Jiddah
Mecca
Medina
Dates
Sheep
Millet
Cattle

Arabian oryx
Bedouin tent
Great Sandy Desert (An Nafud)
Wild horses
Hamadyas baboon
Arabian Desert
Watermelons
Wheat
Dates
Coffee

Barley
Wheat
Water tower
Water tower
SAUDI ARABIA
Everyday clothes

KUWAIT
Kuwait
Oil
Gas
Riyadh

Persian Gulf
Oil
Gas
BAHRAIN

QATAR
Doha
Oil
Abu Dhabi
UNITED ARAB EMIRATES
Gas
Oil

Four-wheel drive car
Oil
Sheep
Dubai
Oil
(Oman)
Gulf of Oman
Muscat

Copper
Chador veil
Goats
Nomad herders
Oil tankers

Camel racing
Coconuts
Goats
Making pots
OMAN
Dolphin

Sidewinder snake
Desert jerboa
The Empty Quarter (Al Rub al Khali)
Limes
Dates
Oil

Dhow fishing boat
Sardines

Arabian Sea
Reef shark
N
E
S
W
SOCOTRA (Yemen)

Dromedary camel
Goats
YEMEN
Rice
Cotton
Sheep
Sana
Millet
Aden
Manta ray
Whale shark

ETHIOPIA
SOMALIA

This distance is the same as 340 miles (550km) on the ground.

29

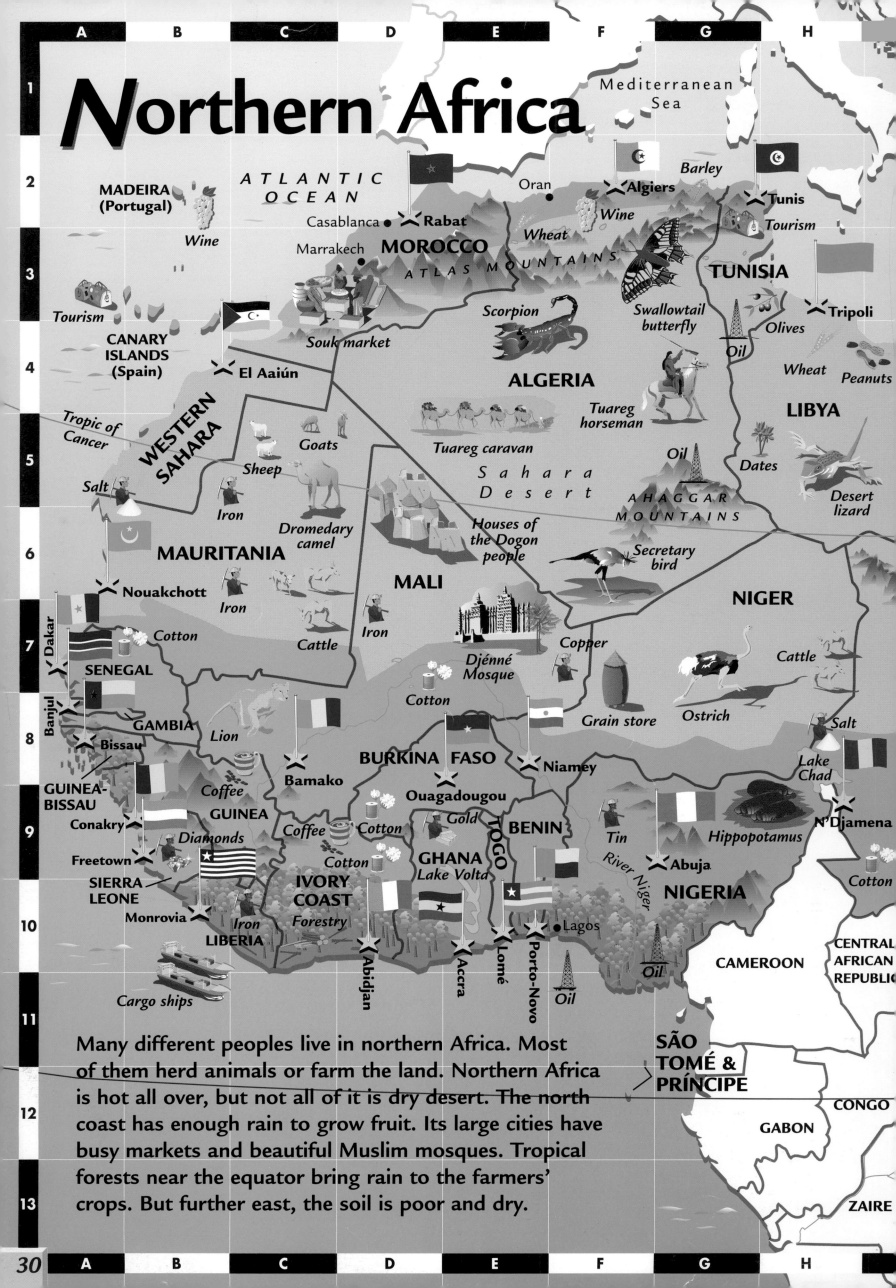

Northern Africa

A B C D E F G H

Mediterranean Sea

ATLANTIC OCEAN

MADEIRA (Portugal)

Wine

Oran

Algiers

Barley

Tunis

Tourism

Casablanca

Rabat

Wine

Wheat

Marrakech

MOROCCO

TUNISIA

ATLAS MOUNTAINS

Tourism

CANARY ISLANDS (Spain)

Scorpion

Swallowtail butterfly

Tripoli

Olives

Oil

El Aaiún

ALGERIA

Wheat

Peanuts

Tropic of Cancer

WESTERN SAHARA

Tuareg horseman

LIBYA

Salt

Goats

Sheep

Tuareg caravan

Oil

Dates

Iron

Sahara Desert

AHAGGAR MOUNTAINS

Desert lizard

Dromedary camel

MAURITANIA

Houses of the Dogon people

Secretary bird

Nouakchott

Iron

MALI

NIGER

Dakar

Cotton

Iron

Copper

Cattle

SENEGAL

Cattle

Djénné Mosque

Ostrich

Banjul

Cotton

Grain store

Salt

GAMBIA

Lion

Lake Chad

Bissau

Bamako

BURKINA FASO

Niamey

GUINEA-BISSAU

Coffee

Ouagadougou

Tin

Hippopotamus

N'Djamena

Conakry

GUINEA

Coffee

Cotton

Gold

BENIN

River Niger

Diamonds

Cotton

GHANA

TOGO

Abuja

Freetown

Cotton

Lake Volta

Cotton

SIERRA LEONE

IVORY COAST

NIGERIA

Monrovia

Iron

Forestry

Lagos

LIBERIA

Abidjan

Accra

Lomé

Porto-Novo

Oil

CENTRAL AFRICAN REPUBLIC

Cargo ships

CAMEROON

SÃO TOMÉ & PRÍNCIPE

CONGO

GABON

Many different peoples live in northern Africa. Most of them herd animals or farm the land. Northern Africa is hot all over, but not all of it is dry desert. The north coast has enough rain to grow fruit. Its large cities have busy markets and beautiful Muslim mosques. Tropical forests near the equator bring rain to the farmers' crops. But further east, the soil is poor and dry.

ZAIRE

A B C D E F G H

EUROPE

TURKEY

N
W **E**
S

Factfile

The Suez Canal joins the Red Sea to the Mediterranean Sea. It is one of the busiest waterways in the world.

The Sahara Desert is about as big as the United States of America! It is the largest desert in the world.

Ghana had so much gold that the first Europeans to discover it called it the "Gold Coast."

The Nile crocodile has been hunted so much that it is now in danger of dying out.

Lemons
Dates
Oil
Oranges
Olives
Oil
Oil
Gas
Gas
Oil

Alexandria
Oil
Suez Canal
Cairo

Pyramids
Sphinx
Wheat
Corn

EGYPT
Cotton

Dates
Carpet weaving
Lake Nasser
Sailing

Bedouin tent

River Nile

Scorpion
Crocodile

Red Sea

SAUDI ARABIA

This distance is the same as 600 miles (960km) on the ground.

Village huts

SUDAN
Khartoum

ERITREA
Asmera

YEMEN

CHAD
Dates
Cattle

Herding cattle

Cattle
Sheep

Cargo ships

DJIBOUTI
Djibouti

SOMALIA
Cattle

Sheep
Elephant
Baobab tree

Cotton
Cheetah

Addis Ababa

ETHIOPIA
ETHIOPIAN HIGHLANDS

Hamadyas baboon

Goats
Sheep

Mogadishu

Bananas
Equator

INDIAN OCEAN

FACT FINDER

▶ Which tombs near Cairo were built over 4,000 years ago for ancient Egyptian kings? (See square K 4.)

▶ Which African mammal is the fastest sprinter in the world? (See square L 10.)

▶ What is the name of the world's longest river, which flows through northern Africa? (See square L 7.)

Southern Africa

Southern Africa is a vast land of grasslands, rainforests, mountains and deserts. The plains of Kenya and Tanzania are famous for their huge herds of animals. Further west, in the rainforests, there are gorillas, monkeys and tropical birds. Many different peoples live in Africa. Most of them farm in small villages, but the cities are growing. Many countries mine copper and gold. Some mine diamonds too.

Factfile

Southern Africa is home to the black rhino and the mountain gorilla, two of the world's most endangered animals.

Southern Africa has large areas of rainforest. Altogether, about one quarter of the world's forests grow in southern Africa.

South Africa is the world's largest producer of gold.

This distance is the same as 450 miles (725km) on the ground.

Tropic of Cancer

Equator

NIGERIA

Coffee

Yams

CAMEROON

Forestry

Yaoundé

Oil

CHAD

CENTRAL AFRICAN REPUBLIC

Cassava

Yams

Cotton

Forestry

Bangui

Diamonds

SUDAN

ETHIOPIA

SOMALIA

UGANDA

Kampala

Coffee

KENYA

Office blocks

Nairobi

Flamingoes

Lake Victoria

Coffee

Tea

Coffee

RWANDA

Kigali

Coffee

BURUNDI

Bujumbura

Mt Kilimanjaro

Elephants

Lake Tanganyika

Balloon

Chimpanzee

River Zaire

Mountain gorilla

ZAIRE

Diamonds

Okapi

Dug-out canoes

African gray parrot

River Kasai

Cassava

CONGO

Forestry

Crocodile

Brazzaville

Kinshasa

GABON

Libreville

Forestry

Oil

CABINDA (Angola)

Oil

EQUATORIAL GUINEA

Malabo

Oil

Dodoma

Zanzibar Island

Tourism

Dar es Salaam

SEYCHELLES

N

W

E

S

Equator

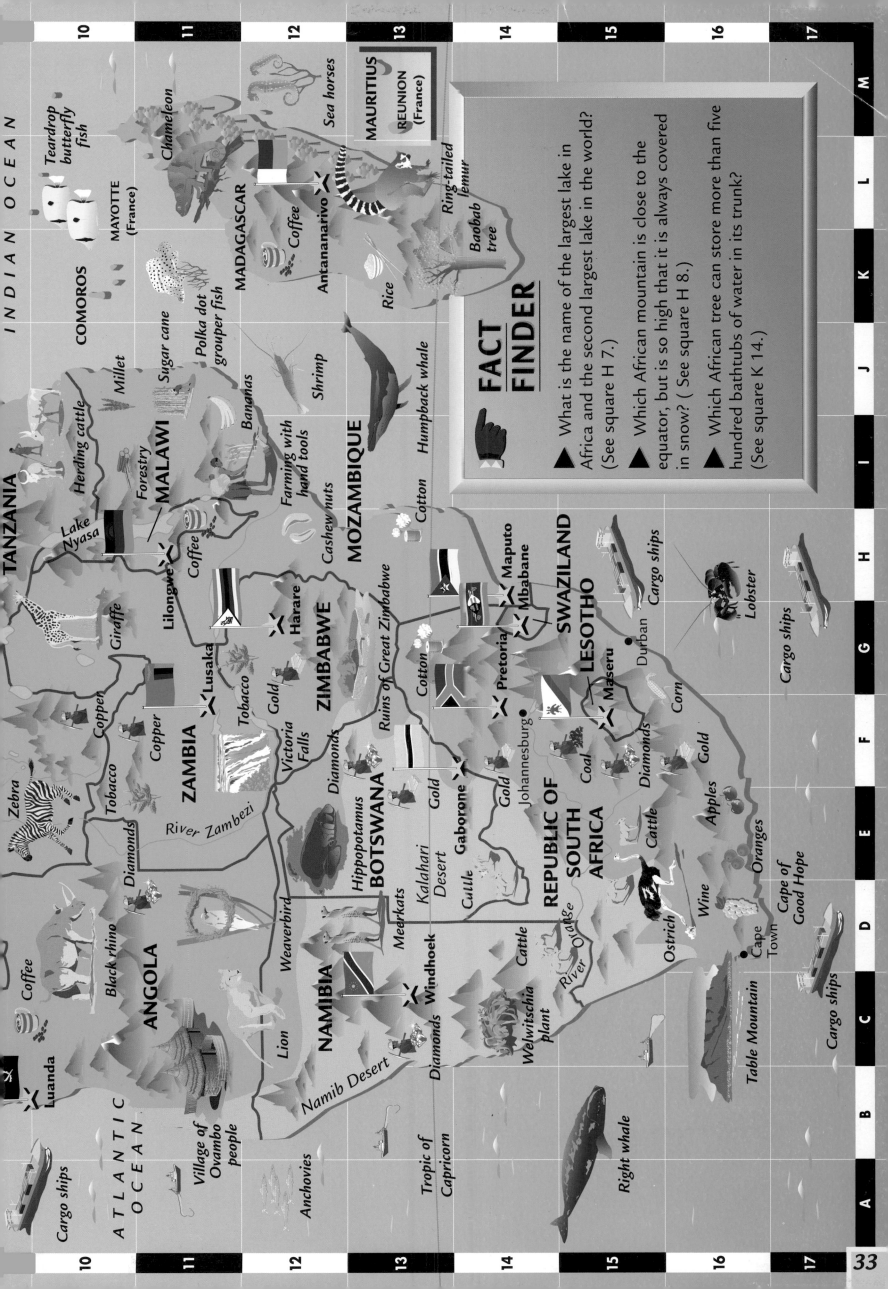

FACT FINDER

☞ What is the name of the largest lake in Africa and the second largest lake in the world? (See square H 7.)

☞ Which African mountain is close to the equator, but is so high that it is always covered in snow? (See square H 8.)

☞ Which African tree can store more than five hundred bathtubs of water in its trunk? (See square K 14.)

INDIAN OCEAN

Teardrop butterfly fish

Chameleon

MAYOTTE (France)

COMOROS

MAURITIUS

Sea horses

REUNION (France)

Sugar cane

Polka dot grouper fish

Millet

MADAGASCAR

Coffee

Antananarivo

Ring-tailed lemur

Baobab tree

Rice

Bananas

Shrimp

Herding cattle

Forestry

MALAWI

Farming with hand tools

MOZAMBIQUE

Cashew nuts

Humpback whale

TANZANIA

Lake Nyasa

Coffee

Lilongwe

Cotton

Maputo

Giraffe

Harare

Mbabane

SWAZILAND

Zebra

Lusaka

Tobacco

ZIMBABWE

Ruins of Great Zimbabwe

Cotton

Pretoria

LESOTHO

Cargo ships

Copper

Gold

Maseru

Durban

Copper

ZAMBIA

Victoria Falls

Diamonds

Cotton

Gold

Corn

Lobster

Tobacco

River Zambezi

Gold

Johannesburg

Coal

Diamonds

Gold

Cargo ships

Diamonds

Black rhino

Hippopotamus

BOTSWANA

Gaborone

REPUBLIC OF SOUTH AFRICA

Cattle

Apples

Coffee

ANGOLA

Kalahari Desert

Cattle

Wine

Oranges

Luanda

Lion

Weaverbird

Meerkats

Windhoek

Ostrich

Cape Town

Cape of Good Hope

Village of Ovambo people

NAMIBIA

River Orange

Table Mountain

Anchovies

Welwitschia plant

Cattle

Cargo ships

Namib Desert

Tropic of Capricorn

Diamonds

Right whale

ATLANTIC OCEAN

Cargo ships

33

Southern Asia

Southern Asia stretches from the Himalayan Mountains in the north of India to the island of Sri Lanka in the south. The weather is mostly hot and dry, although for several months there are heavy rains. More than a billion people live in southern Asia. Most people live in villages and farm the land, but many are beginning to move to the cities. The cities are a mixture of old and new, with modern buildings next to ancient temples and palaces. The busy streets are packed with cars, trucks and buses, but also with ox-carts and elephants.

👉 FACT FINDER

▲ Which white marble temple, decorated with precious stones, was built in the 17th century by an Indian emperor as a burial place for his wife? (See square G 8.)

▲ In India, which animal is used to help people with heavy work such as moving timber? (See square F 11.)

▲ What are Pakistan, Afghanistan and India all famous for weaving? (See squares C 6, C 9 and F 7.)

▲ In India, which three-wheeled vehicle that looks a little like a bicycle is often used to carry people from one place to another? (See square I 10.)

TURKMENISTAN

UZBEKISTAN

TAJIKISTAN

CHINA

Bactrian camel

Cattle

Blue Mosque

Carpet weaving

Kabul

AFGHANISTAN

River Helmand

Milking goats

Cotton

Wheat

Rubies

Peaches

Goats

Quetta

PAKISTAN

Thar Desert

Cotton

Wheat

Sheep

River Indus

Goats

Wheat

Shah Faisal Mosque

Islamabad

Lahore

Sugar cane

Carpet weaving

KARAKORAM

Cobra

Cattle

Making silk

Snow leopard

RANGE

Goats

Wheat

Yak

HIMALAYAN MOUNTAINS

Mountain peaks

Mt Everest

Delhi

Taj Mahal

NEPAL

Kathmandu

Sugar cane

Rice

Thimpu

BHUTAN

Tea

River Brahmaputra

Buddhist monk

Tea

Oil

Indian rhino

34

MYANMAR

Dhaka

BANGLADESH

Chittagong
Calcutta

Lobster

Car building

Reef shark

ANDAMAN
ISLANDS
(India)

Making
silk

Crocodile

Iron

Rice

Polka dot
grouper fish

Coral

NICOBAR
ISLANDS
(India)

N

E

W

S

Equator

Humpback
whale

River Ganges

INDIA

Coal

Bicycle
rickshaw

Rice

Dolphins

Vishakhapatnam

Water
buffalo

INDIAN OCEAN

Forestry

Black bear

Coal

Classical
Indian
dancing

Madras

Pearls

Sardines

SRI
LANKA

Nagpur

VINHDAYA RANGE

Working
elephant

River Godavari

Cotton

Goods
truck

Car building

Coconuts

Rice

Tea

Colombo

Peacock

Hyderabad

Gold

Tiger

Bangalore

Cattle

Ahmadabad
Dromedary
camels

River Narmada

Oil

Making
clothes

Black panther

Millet

Iron

Cochin

Ship
building

Scuba diving

Outrigger fishing boat

Wheat

Sheep

Peanuts

Cotton

Bombay

Film
making ♪>♫

Steam
train

Tourism

Shrimp

Coral

Clown fish

MALDIVE
ISLANDS

Carpet
weaving

Karachi

Film
making ♪>♫

Dhow fishing boat

Blue whale

Millet

Oil

Tropic of Cancer

Herring

This distance is the same as
360 miles (575km) on the ground.

Factfile

♪>♫

More films are made in southern
Asia than anywhere else in the
world. India makes over 700
films a year.

The mountains of southern
Asia are home to the snow
leopard, one of the world's
most endangered animals.

Southern Asia is the world's
largest producer of tea.

35

Eastern Asia

Eastern Asia is made up of China, Mongolia, Japan, North and South Korea, Taiwan and Hong Kong. It is a vast land with mountains and deserts in the north and west. Most people live further east, where there is more rain and good farmland. China is a huge country. Many people are farmers and live in the countryside. In Japan, most people live in cities. They work in factories and offices.

RUSSIA

This distance is the same as 280 miles (450km) on the ground.

Goats

Red deer

ALTAI MOUNTAINS

Ulan Bator

Yurt

M O N G

TIEN SHAN MOUNTAINS

Wolf

Copper

Coal

Gob

Oil

Cotton

Goats

Iron

Rice

Sheep

Bactrian camel

Wheat

Cotton

Sand grouse

Wild horses

Wild horses

Cotton

Takla Makan Desert

Oil

Sheep

Vulture

Gas

Cotton

Great Wall of China

PAKISTAN

K2 (Mt Godwin Austen)

Tai Chi exercises

Salt mining

TIBET

Calligraphy

Wild boar

Snow leopard

C H I N A

INDIA

HIMALAYAN MOUNTAINS

Yak

Cattle

Goats

Sheep

Pigs

Buddhist monk

Chengdu

Mountain peaks

▲ Mt Everest

Potala Palace

Great Buddha

BHUTAN

INDIA

N

MYANMAR

Stone forest

W

E

Tobacco

Tea

LAOS

S

THAILAND

FACT FINDER

► Which ancient exercises do many Chinese people perform every morning to keep themselves healthy? (See E 7.)

► Which wall is about 4,000 miles (6,400km) long and was built over 500 years ago to protect China from northern invaders? (See square H 6.)

► What is the name of the tent traveling herders in Mongolia live in to protect themselves from the heat and cold of the plains? (See square G 3.)

Factfile

Tibet's mountains and plateau are the highest in the world.

More people live in China than in any other country. It contains about one-fifth of all the people in the world.

Japan catches the most fish in the world. Along with rice, it is the main food eaten by the Japanese people.

Southeast Asia

1
2

TAIWAN

Scuba diving

CHINA

Tropic of Cancer

Coral

Clown fish

Coral

S o u t h

C h i n a

S e a

Stilt house

LUZON

Coal

Wild boar

MYANMAR

Water buffalo

Hanoi

Copper

Manila

Working elephant

LAOS

PHILIP

Rice

Vientiane

THAILAND

River Mekong

VIETNAM

Tiger

Cargo ships

River Irrawaddy

Silver

Making silk

Rice

Cassava

Herring

Coral

Floating market

Anchovies

Gold   Yangon

Bangkok

Sardines

INDIAN OCEAN

Angkor Wat

Corn

Phnom Penh

Ho Chi Minh City

Pearls

Oil

Bandar Seri Begawan

CAMBODIA

Rice

Tuna

BRUNEI

Reef sharks

Lobster

Tourism

Gas

Oil

Making rubber

Leatherback turtle

Rice

M A L A Y S I A

Polka dot grouper fish

Malayan tapir

Iron

Forestry

Orang-utan

Gas

Coral

Tourism

Kuala Lumpur

Office blocks

SINGAPORE

BORNEO

Oil

Forestry

Volcanoes

Oil

I N D O

SUMATRA

Gas

Cargo ships

FACT FINDER

▶ What is the name of the world's largest lizard? It can grow more than 10 feet (3m) long and lives only in Indonesia. (See square J 11.)

▶ Which temple in Cambodia is one of the architectural wonders of the world? It was built over 800 years ago to honor the Hindu god, Vishnu. (See square D 7.)

Volcanoes

Orchid

Rafflesia flower

Jakarta   JAVA

Volcanoes

Tea

Sea horses

Teardrop butterfly fish

Coral

Southeast Asia is made up of a narrow strip of land and thousands of small islands. The area has high mountains, tropical forests and river valleys. The weather is hot and wet all year round. Many of the people are farmers, who grow rice and corn for food, and rubber and coffee to sell. But the cities are growing, and more people are finding work in factories and offices.

This distance is the same as 500 miles (800km) on the ground.

Factfile

Rubber is made from the sap of the rubber tree. Southeast Asia produces over three-quarters of the world's rubber.

There are more active volcanoes in southeast Asia than in any other area of the world. The ash left behind from volcanic eruptions helps to make the soil good for farming.

The country of Indonesia is made up of over 13,600 islands. It is the biggest chain of islands in the world and has the world's fourth largest population.

PINES

Bicycle rickshaw

Coconuts

MINDANAO

N O R T H

P A C I F I C

O C E A N

Outrigger fishing boat

Equator

Tuna

Bird of paradise

Coconuts

Sponge

Gas *Oil*

IRIAN JAYA (Indonesia)

Coconuts

MALUKU

PAPUA NEW GUINEA

Shrimp

Bananas

Cloves

Tree kangaroo

★ *Port Moresby*

Echidna

SULAWESI

Flying lizard

Crab

Humpback whale

Coffee

N E S I A

Manta ray

N

Komodo dragon

TIMOR

FLORES

E

BALI

SUMBA

Shrimp

W

Tourism

AUSTRALIA

S

Dolphins

Tropic of Capricorn

Australia, New Zealand
and the Pacific Islands

The Pacific Ocean is dotted with thousands of islands. Many people live in villages and grow crops or hunt for fish. Australia is an island too, but it is so big that it is a continent. Most Australians live in cities or farm land near the coast. A lot of Australia is hot and dry, but it has mountains and rainforests too. It also has animals and plants that are not found anywhere else.

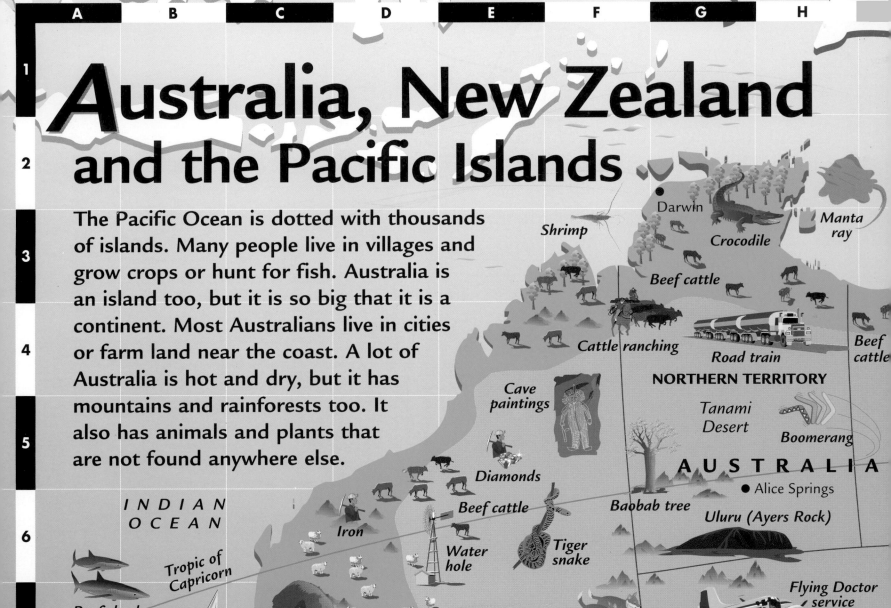

Darwin, Shrimp, Crocodile, Manta ray, Beef cattle, Cattle ranching, Road train, NORTHERN TERRITORY, Cave paintings, Tanami Desert, Boomerang, Beef cattle, Diamonds, AUSTRALIA, Baobab tree, Alice Springs, Beef cattle, Uluru (Ayers Rock), Water hole, Tiger snake, INDIAN OCEAN, Flying Doctor service, Tropic of Capricorn, Reef sharks, Emu, Sheep, Camels, Dingoes, SOUTH AUSTRALIA, Lake Eyre, Sailing, WESTERN AUSTRALIA, Great Victoria Desert, Opals, Coober Pedy, Echidna, Gold, Budgerigar, Wombat, Perth, Wave Rock, Koala, Orange, Adelaide, Wine, Lobster, Dolphin

FACT FINDER

▶ Which lake in southern Australia is dry for most of the year and fills with water only after heavy rains? (See square H 8.)

▶ Which mammal has a furry body and feeds milk to its young, but has a duck's bill and hatches its young from eggs? This mammal is only found in Australia. (See square J 9.)

▶ Many of Australia's rocks are very old. Can you find one that is shaped like a wave and is over 3,000 million years old? (See square D 9.)

Factfile

The Great Barrier Reef off the east coast of Australia is the biggest coral reef in the world.

Nearly half of the world's 3,000 languages are spoken by people in the Pacific Islands.

Australia is the world's flattest continent.

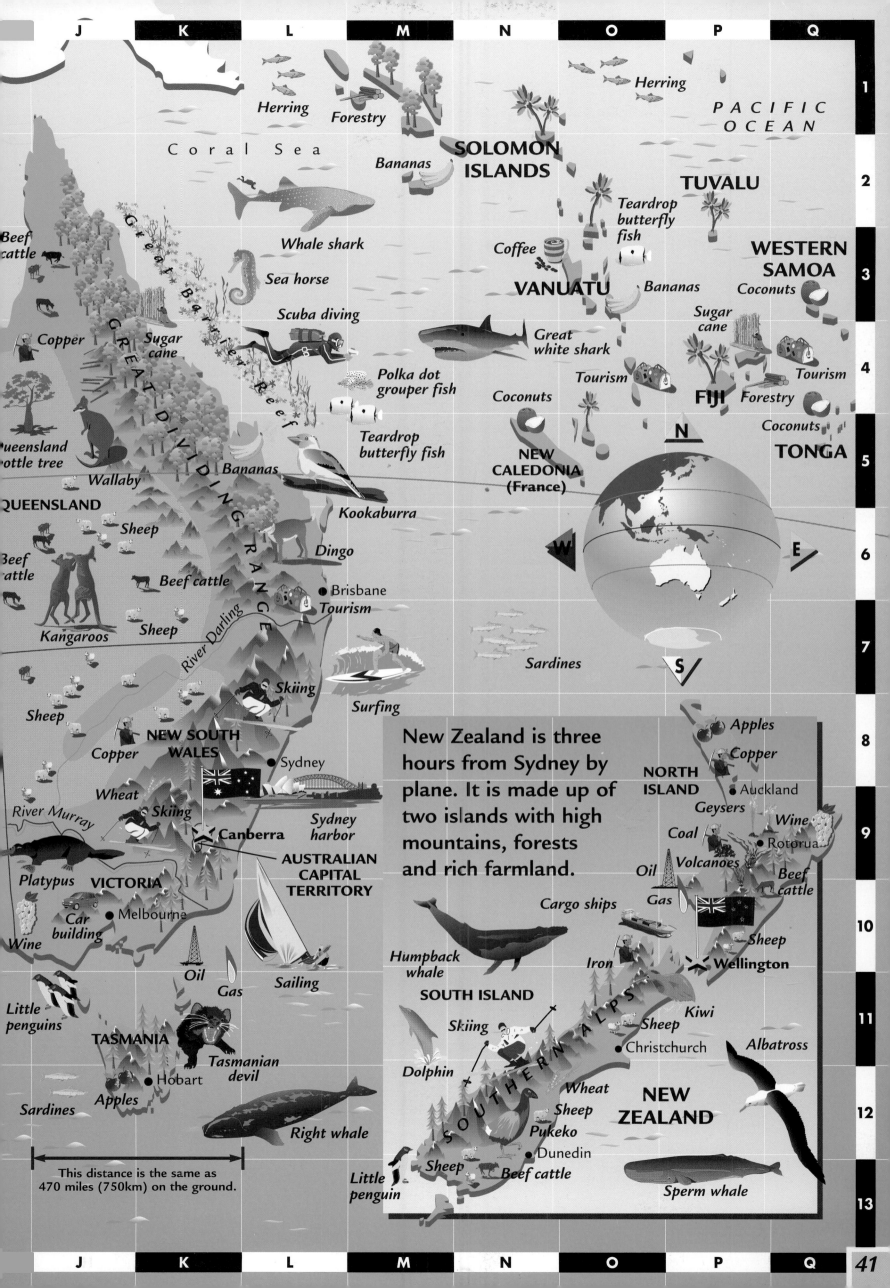

Fascinating facts

On these pages, you can discover interesting facts about the world. Look up the names of the places in the index and find out where they are on the maps in this atlas.

Where in the world is...

...the hottest place?
Al Aziziyah in Libya. The highest temperature ever recorded was 136°F (58°C).

In Al Aziziyah, you could fry an egg on a sun-baked rock.

...the coldest place?
Vostock in Antarctica. The lowest temperature ever recorded was -129°F. (-89°C). This is over three times as cold as inside a deep freeze.

...the wettest place?
Mawsynram in India, where nearly 40 feet (12m) of rain falls each year. This is enough to cover a three-story building.

...the driest place?
Atacama Desert in Chile, where it has rained only a few times in the last 400 years.

Which country is the...

...biggest country?
Russia, which is 6,592,850 square miles (17,075,400sq km).

...smallest country?
Vatican City, which is 109 acres (44 hectares).

If Russia were the size of a soccer field, the Vatican City would be the size of a small stamp.

...emptiest country?
Mongolia, which has a huge desert and towering mountains. There are only a few towns which are far apart.

...most crowded country?
Monaco, which is a tiny country in Europe. It has an orchestra larger than its army.

Where is the...

...highest mountain in the world?
Mount Everest in the Himalayas, in Nepal. It is about 29,028 ft. (8,848m) high—over nine times as tall as the highest waterfall in the world.

29,028 feet

...highest waterfall in the world?
Angel Falls, in Venezuela. It has a total drop of about 3,212 ft. (979m)—over twice as high as the tallest building in North America.

3,212 feet

...highest building in North America?
Sears Tower, US. It is about 1,454 ft. (443m) tall—nearly four times taller than the tallest geyser in the world.

1,454 feet

...highest geyser in the world?
Steamboat Geyser, US, has reached a height of about 380 ft. (115m)— slightly taller than the tallest tree in the world.

380 feet

...highest tree in the world?
A redwood tree in California, US. It is about 368 ft. (112m) high—over 40 times taller than the tallest person in the world.

368 feet

Who was the world's tallest person?
An American called Robert Pershing Wadlow was the world's tallest person. He was over 8 ft., 11 in. (2.7m) tall.

FACT FINDER

Find these record-breaking places in the atlas.

▶ The highest mountain (page 34, square J 8)

▶ The tallest waterfall (page 20, square E 4)

▶ The longest river (page 31, square L 7)

▶ The driest place (page 21, square E 9)

W

London

New York

E

Tokyo

What time is it?

Across the world, at the same moment, clocks show different times. This is because the world is divided into time zones. All time is measured from Greenwich, London, UK. When you cross a time zone to the east of Greenwich, time is one hour ahead. When you cross a time zone to the west of Greenwich, time is one hour behind.

The letters *am* stand for ante meridian, which means the hours from midnight until mid-day, or the morning. The letters *pm* stand for post meridian, which means the hours from mid-day until midnight, or the afternoon and evening.

If it is 12pm in London, what time is it in New York and Tokyo?

Land and sea

Imagine the world as a cake. Most of the cake would be oceans and seas, and one small slice would be the land. Most of the slice of land would be desert, rainforest, mountains, ice and grassland. Less than half the slice would be places where people can live and farm. In this atlas, you can find the biggest rainforest on page 20, see square H 5, and the biggest desert on page 30, see square E 5.

Which are the three longest rivers?

The River Nile in North Africa is 4,145 miles (6,671km) long. You could walk along its length in over four months.

The River Amazon in South America is 4,000 miles (6,437km) long. You could run along its length in over two months.

The River Yangtze in China is 3,915 miles (6,300km) long. You could cycle fast from one end to the other in just over one month.

Index

This index lists all the places on the maps in this atlas. The page number tells you which map to go to and the grid reference tells you where the place is on the map. You can find out how to look for grid references on page 9.